The Sin of Wages:

Where the Conventional Pay System Has Led Us and How to Find a Way Out

William B. Abernathy, Ph.D.

Copyright 1996 © William B. Abernathy, Ph.D.

Library of Congress Catalog Card Number: 96-92835

ISBN 0-9655276-0-3

Published in the United States of America
PerfSys Press

About the Author

Bill Abernathy received his master's degree in Experimental Psychology from the George Peabody College of Vanderbilt University and his doctorate in Organizational Psychology from Ohio State University. Bill served as an Associate Professor of Psychology at Ohio University and with the performance improvement firm of Edward J. Feeney and Associates. In 1981, he founded Abernathy & Associates.

About Abernathy & Associates

Abernathy & Associates assists clients in the design and implementation of the *Total Performance System* as developed by Bill and outlined in Section II. TPS provides a company an integrated, organization-wide performance management and incentive pay system.

Abernathy & Associates provides outsourced administration for the Total Performance System. Clients transmit performance data to A&A who prepares an Executive Summary, performance scorecards and charts for each employee, a client network Data Viewer, and an incentive payroll. A&A's advisory service ensures the client's performance system remains valid, provides continuous improvements, and ensures a good return on the incentive pay investment.

To learn more about Abernathy & Associates and the *Total Performance System* contact:

Abernathy & Associates
665 Oakleaf Office Lane
Memphis, TN 38117
(901) 763-2122
Fax (901) 763-3086

Or visit our web site at www.abernathyassociates.com

Acknowledgments

The ideas presented in Section I have their foundation in the behavioral theory of the Harvard psychologist, B.F. Skinner. Though often controversial, Dr. Skinner remained consistent throughout his life in his effort to apply the methods of science to understanding human behavior. It is my hope that this book helps extend his approach and theory to employee behavior in organizations.

The term "Total Performance System" was coined by Dale Brethower in 1972 to describe "an adaptive system comprised of a set of components which, when operational, are sufficient to improve or maintain the performance of the system."[1]. I use the term here to describe a specific set of interrelated components that include the performance scorecard, profit-indexed performance pay, and positive leadership.

Section II describes this system which has evolved over twenty years of working with business leaders and their organizations. Unfortunately, it isn't possible here to adequately recognize each person and their organization's contribution to the development of the system. However, the following individuals have played an especially unique role.

I wish to thank Hall McAdams, past chairman of Union National Bank, for taking a risk and allowing a displaced college professor to tinker around in his bank for fifteen years. Without this "laboratory" and his, and his staff's, cooperation, I would have been unable to start my work.

Ed Feeney and John Staelin of Edward J. Feeney and Associates introduced me to business and consulting. My work with them helped me formulate some of my ideas about Positive Leadership. I also wish to thank Hawley Brooks and Ed Wallace whom I worked with for several years at Sovran Bank. It was there that many of the performance pay and behavioral system concepts described in the latter part of this book were spawned.

Last, I wish to recognize Joe Savage, Gene Williams and the staff of Abernathy & Associates for their substantial contributions to the ideas presented here, and my wife, Conie, for enabling me to pursue my ideas with her unwavering support.

[1] Dale M. Brethower, Behavioral Analysis in Business and Industry: A Total Performance System (Kalamazoo, MI: Behaviordelia, Inc., 1972.) p. 4.

Table of Contents

Section I:
The Seven Sins of Wages

Chapter 1: The Evolution of the Pay Crisis

A BRIEF HISTORY OF EVENTS THAT LED US TO OUR CURRENT ORGAN-IZATIONAL PAY AND MANAGEMENT SYSTEM, AND AN OVERVIEW OF THE SEVEN "SINS" OF THIS SYSTEM.

Webster's defines a "system" as "an orderly, interconnected, complex arrangement of parts." Our country's economy is based loosely on a free enterprise system. This system supports entrepreneurs, the self-employed and business owners, but does not extend to employees who work for others. Employees function in a different system than do their organization's ownership.

The free enterprise system rewards innovation and risk-taking. But many organizations are bureaucratic systems that discourage employee innovation and risk-taking. The free enterprise system rewards results and personal accountability. But the bureaucratic system often rewards form over function and shifts accountability from labor to management. How did this happen?

The rise of individual enterprise. Before the 18th century, there was almost no expansion of wealth or income. Even the most advanced countries, such as the Netherlands, experienced at best a one percent annual increase in national wealth. The birth of Capitalism in 1776 with the publication of Adam Smith's *An Inquiry into the Nature and Causes of the Wealth of Nations* marked a turning point in human productivity.

Smith's economic theory was based on what he called man's "self-love." As he wrote: "It is not from the benevolence of the butcher, the brewer or the baker that we expect our dinner, but from their regard for their own self interest." Smith's views spread to the extent that production and consumption in Britain increased a staggering 1,600 percent during the 19th century. [1]

Small shopkeepers, artisans and independent farmers sprung up across the country as free enterprise became a way of life. A new optimism that anyone could improve his condition replaced the thousands of years of class distinction and privilege that had repressed the working class and individual enterprise. The 19th century in the United States was a period of almost boundless optimism for the average worker. Opportunities were seemingly unlimited if one had the initiative and perseverance to capitalize on them.

As I finish this book, the Presidential campaign is in full force. There is much talk about the "American Dream." I recall when the American Dream meant the opportunity to pursue your own goals, your own way. The politicians have perverted the dream to mean new homes and cars and a risk-free world. What happened to the real "American Dream"?

Causes of the decline of individual enterprise.

1) Mass production. During this same era a second development facilitated this prosperity, but also sowed the seeds for the death of individual enterprise for the common worker — Eli Whitney's mass production.

> Whitney's standardized parts could be fitted by drones with no other skills.... Whitney's principle of mass production through uniform molds transferred the skill from the man to the machine. His factory system entailed small teams doing only one task of an

assembly routine. It was sufficiently revolutionary to be called "the Whitney System" and then, in Europe, "the American System." [2]

2) *Wages.* Henry Ford is credited with introducing hourly wages on a large scale. Since then, pay-for-time has become the standard for compensating employees in an organization. The adverse impact of this approach to pay is pervasive.

3) *Information Age.* The assembly line removed workers from the fruits of their labors. This separation of the worker from his product widened again with the entrance of what John Naisbitt terms the "Information Society."

In 1950 only about 17 percent of us worked in information jobs. Now more than 60 percent of us work with information as programmers, teachers, clerks, secretaries, accountants, stock brokers, managers, insurance people, bureaucrats, lawyers, bankers, and technicians... Most Americans spend their time creating, processing, or distributing information.... [3]

The worker has moved rapidly from a feudal system, through a free enterprise system, to today's wage and salary based mass production of information. In so doing, much of the independence and ambition found in the highly successful entrepreneurial foundations of our country were lost.

The farmer, shopkeeper and artisan of the 19th century reaped the benefits of what they sowed and conversely suffered the consequences of poor performance. Specialized "paper shuffling" often lacks any connectedness to the final product. The individual worker is so removed from the ultimate outcome of his day-to-day work, no sense of personal accomplishment or direct personal benefit is gained from good performance.

4) Bureaucratic organization. With the assembly line, organizations' grew larger and the average worker became only a cog in the machinery of the organization — what William H. Whyte, Jr., termed "The Organization Man" in 1957.

> In current retrospect the turn of the century seems a golden age of individualism; yet by the 1880s the corporation had already shown the eventual bureaucratic direction it was going to take. As institutions grew in size and became more stratified, they made all too apparent inconsistencies which formerly could be ignored.
>
> One of the key assumptions of the Protestant ethic had been that success was due neither to luck nor to the environment but only to one's natural qualities — if men grew rich, it was because they deserved to. But the big organization became a standing taunt to this dream of individual success. Quite obviously to anyone who worked in a big organization, those who survived best were not necessarily the fittest but, in more cases than not, those who by birth and personal connectedness had the breaks.[4]

Whyte argued that the Protestant ethic of self-reliance and improvement was essentially a myth in corporate America. There is little in his argument that has changed since then. Much of the formal groundwork for the modern corporate bureaucracy is found in the writings of Max Weber at the turn of the century. Weber described six characteristics of the large organization:

-specific activities and duties (division of labor) are defined and the extent of authority delimited by rules.

-a chain of command exists to promote informational and decision flow within the organization.

-ownership is separated from management.

-management is distinct from other types of activities.

-management is a full-time activity.

-managers follow specific rules which are applied uniformly and unemotionally in order to fairly regulate each case. [5]

5) *A loss of connectedness in the workplace.* It is common for people to confuse the benefits the workplace offers with the satisfaction derived from the work itself. A good example of this confusion is the debate over merit pay for teachers. The union's position is that the salary is inadequate and should be increased to retain excellent teachers rather than pay on teacher merit. This view misses the point. The absolute amount of pay is a separate issue from how the pay is earned. What is important, and overlooked, is establishing a *connection* between performance and organizational rewards. The behavioral psychologist B.F. Skinner eloquently described this relationship:

> But satisfaction is a limited objective; we are not necessarily happy because we have everything we want. The word "sated" is related to the word sad. Simple abundance, whether in an affluent society, a benevolent climate, or a welfare state, is not enough. When people are supplied according to their needs,

11

regardless of what they are doing, they remain inactive.[6]

The effects of mass production, the wage and salary system, the information age, the bureaucratic organization, and the loss of connectedness between performance and pay has eroded worker initiative and job satisfaction.

The Pay Crisis. Our work force is in the beginnings of a real crisis. Job security has declined and layoffs are commonplace. Wage gains have moved from stagnant to real declines in buying power. Pay reductions were once unheard of and now are grimly accepted. The Fortune 500 companies employed sixteen million workers in 1974 but only twelve million in 1994.

Many reasons are cited including increased healthcare costs and government mandates; the entrance of global competition; and Third World low-paid, highly motivated workers. However, one of the most overlooked problems facing business and labor is our outmoded pay system.

The conventional pay system is characterized by:

1) guaranteed wages and salaries.

2) annual "merit evaluations" and merit pay increases.

3) annual cost-of-living pay increases.

4) market-based pay set by a market survey.

This system came into its current form after World War II when there was a labor shortage and high worldwide demand for products. Conventional pay has become so ingrained in our thinking, it is now difficult to imagine any other way of paying people. However, before the industrial revolution, some 75 percent of Americans were farmers or artisans and not paid a wage or salary. Today over ten percent of the work force is self-employed and a significant number of sales positions are highly commissioned. The concept of paying for time rather than results is, then, relatively new and only one of several options.

It is interesting to speculate what would happen if beings from another planet visited here. If they observed our personnel departments, they would hear about paid hours, time sheet hours, vacation time, sick time, holiday time, overtime, undertime, lost time, compensatory time, time-in-grade and so on. They might conclude that our companies are in the business of manufacturing *time*.

On their planet, workers are paid directly for the products and services they produce. Imagine a meeting where we tried to persuade these beings to adopt our approach to pay. "You should stop paying your workers for what they produce and start paying them for the time they spend producing it."

1.3 The Seven Sins of Conventional "Entitlement Pay"

The following is an overview of the concepts presented in chapters two through eight. These chapters will describe the seven sins of conventional compensation and provide examples from several types of organizations. Chapter 9 will outline problems with conventional alternative pay plans. The remaining five chapters discuss the theory and design of the *Total Performance System* as an alternative to conventional entitlement pay.

1. Fixed-Cost Pay. Pay has come to be viewed as an entitlement by employees. Employees believe they are not only entitled to their current pay, but pay increases each year. This view makes the payroll effectively a fixed cost to the organization that grows at a compound rate over time. When revenues stabilize or decline, profits decrease and layoffs are the only recourse. Employees are risking long-term job insecurity for short-term pay guarantees.

Entitlement pay also reduces the number of people employed and the level of pay. Because pay is essentially guaranteed for life, employers are reluctant to add employees or increase pay when the business is successful for fear of the high fixed expense when revenues stabilize or decline. This entitlement view of pay also necessarily makes labor and management adversaries. Management is tied to profit while the work force is artificially removed from it.

2. Pay for Time. "When you pay for time, you get time. When you pay for results, you get results." Hourly pay is particularly detrimental to employee productivity. Parkinson's law tells us "work expands to fill the time available." When you are paid by the hour it is not in your financial interest to work more efficiently since this will simply result in more tasks being assigned or, worse, a cutback in your hours. Employees living on overtime pay aggravate the problem. I find it amazing that management really expects employees to form teams to develop more efficient processes that will simply result in their having to learn additional jobs for the same pay, or even lose their current jobs.

3. Corporate Socialism. Entitlement pay is unfair to good performers. It pays everyone in the same job or pay grade about the same regardless of their personal contribution. The result is that high performance goes unrewarded and performance drifts toward mediocrity. Entitlement thinking has

14

failed as economic policy and doesn't work any better inside our businesses.

4. Performance-Based Promotions. Conventional pay prevents supervisors and managers from directly and immediately paying a subordinate for a job well done. Tight pay bands reduce even the ability to reward performance through annual pay increases. The consequence is that many supervisors and managers must promote top performers to reward them. This creates competition among employees and forces the best performers out of their jobs and into management. Often, top performers prefer to work independently and do not work well through others. The result is the company loses a good performer and creates a dissatisfied and ineffective manager.

The Peter Principle states "employees rise to the level of their incompetence." I would simply add that the driving force behind this principle is the conventional pay system. We reward employees by promoting them until their performance no longer justifies additional promotions.

5. Management by Perception. Conventional wage and salary systems encourage and support "lazy management" practices that undermine employee effectiveness. Time-oriented pay does not require the ongoing measurement of employee performance results. Because employee performance results are not measured, managers must rely on subjective perceptions to determine who is performing and who is not.

6. Management by Exception. Without an objective performance measurement system, managers have no accurate means for recognizing or rewarding improvement and must therefore manage exceptions. In practice, acceptable performance

15

is largely ignored but failures to perform are "managed." In this system, employees don't work to earn their pay, they work to avoid losing it.

7. Entitlement Thinking. Fifty years of guaranteed pay have created an "entitlement culture" in which employees believe they are owed their pay regardless of personal or company performance. The technical term for pay, *compensation*, is revealing. We are compensated for going to work rather than working to *earn* a living. Entitlement thinking has created a nation of risk-averse employees who refuse accountability and are unwilling to accept the cold fact that without a successful business there can be no pay.

References

[1] *Time,* April 21, 1980

[2] Allistair Cooke. *America.* New York: Alfred A. Knoph, 1977.

[3] John Naisbitt. *Megatrends: Ten New Directions Transforming Our Lives.* New York: Warner Books, 1982.

[4] William H. Whyte, Jr. *The Organization Man.* New York: Doubleday & Co., 1957.

[5] Robert L. Treuathan & M. Gene Newport. *Management: Functions and Behaviors.* Dallas, TX: Business Publications, Inc., 1976.

[6] B.F. Skinner. *Contingencies of Reinforcement: A Theoretical Analysis.* New York: Appleton-Century-Croft, 1969.

Chapter 2: Fixed-Cost Pay

2.1

THERE ARE THREE PROBLEMS CAUSED BY PAY SYSTEMS THAT GUAR-ANTEE A FIXED WAGE OR SALARY REGARDLESS OF THE PROFIT OF THE ORGANIZATION: A COMPOUND-GROWTH PAYROLL, A FIXED EXPENSE PAYROLL, AND A FAILURE OF THE CONVENTIONAL PAY SYSTEM TO ALIGN EMPLOYEE GOALS WITH THE ORGANIZATION'S. THE SOLUTION OF MOVING TOWARD A PROFIT- INDEXED PAYROLL IS EXPLAINED.

In his book, *The Share Economy* [1], the economist Martin Weitzman argued that conventional "fixed cost" pay systems are bad economics and cause layoffs and unemployment. He recommended indexing employee pay to the profitability of the company to solve these problems. That is, making pay more a variable expense than a fixed one. (The term profit is used as a synonym for net income. The principles and strategies described apply equally to non-profit organizations.)

1) Conventional Pay Increases Annually at a Compound Rate. The conventional entitlement pay system provides employees short-term pay guarantees but puts their jobs at risk over the long term. This long-term risk is created by the effective fixed-cost nature of guaranteed pay and the compound growth of this expense caused by annual pay increases.

Historically, annual pay increases have averaged about five percent across companies. Every year, the payroll increases five percent above the previous year. If sales or price increases fail to keep pace with payroll increases, profit margins shrink. Today, automatic annual price increases are more difficult to sell to customers than they once were. At some point, the only solution is a layoff.

The following chart illustrates what happens to profit margins over a fifteen-year period with five percent annual pay increases and stable revenues. The payroll expense doubles in fifteen years regardless of profitability.

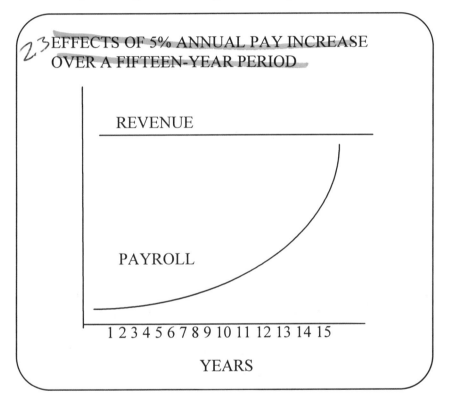

2) Conventional Pay Fails to Adjust for Business Cycles. Fixed expense payrolls don't vary with organizational profitability (the company's ability to pay). The payroll expense remains the same regardless of revenues or work volumes. Most organizations operate in business cycles. Revenue rises and falls in these cycles. A fixed payroll does not adjust for these cycles.

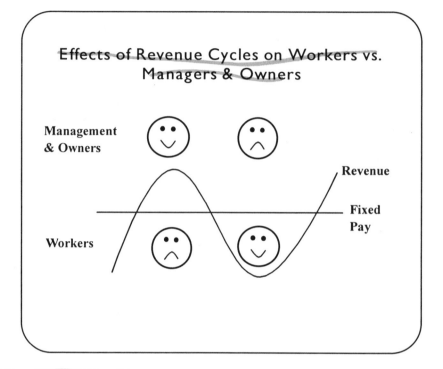

The above chart illustrates that employees are working harder in the peak season for no additional pay. This creates an effort-reward inequity during this season. On the other hand, in the slack season employees are doing less for the same pay they earned in the peak season. In the peak season the employees are unhappy but in the slack season management is unhappy.

While consulting with a company in Bermuda, I discovered that Bermuda's strict immigration created an "overemployment" situation in which there were more jobs than people. The company paid straight wages and salaries. During the tourist season many employees left the company to work for the hotels where they could earn significant tips. When the season was over they returned, since the base wages of the hotels were lower. The company had to rehire them since other employees were not available.

Unfortunately, the company's work volumes were also related to the tourist trade. The outcome was that they had a full staff when they didn't need them, and a reduced staff when they were busiest. A variable-pay system would index employee pay to the profit and work volume variations of the business cycle. Such a system would have corrected the company's problem by paying more during the busy season and less during the off season.

3) Conventional Pay Makes Adversaries of Management and Labor. Fixed-pay systems make ownership and senior managers adversaries of their employees. Owner and senior manager pay is often linked directly to the organization's profitability. In contrast, employee pay is artificially separated from profitability and made a fixed expense. The consequence is that employees and management don't share the same concerns. Employees see expense control, especially labor expense, as working against their best interests. The more employees there are, the less each employee has to do. Employees are also not personally interested in increased revenue in an entitlement pay system. The more revenue the company generates, the more work there is to do for the same pay.

Solution: Index Pay to "Controllable Net Income." Z. Z Ideally, pay would be indexed to true organizational profit. However, many revenues and expenses that make up a company's profit are not under the control of the employee group and shouldn't be. For this reason, we index pay to a subset of profit we term "controllable net income" (see Chapter 12). CNI is made up of revenues and expenses that employees directly or indirectly influence. In cost centers that have no revenue stream, an expense ratio of controllable expenses to volume (cost/unit) can be substituted for a net number. "Uncontrollable" expenses are covered by a "threshold" below which there is no employee performance pay opportunity.

To successfully index pay to profitability, management must be willing to share financial information with employees. In my opinion, they should be sharing this information anyway. How can employees be aligned with company objectives when they are not made aware of how the company makes a profit and how well the company is doing?

A good example of the importance of communication is a performance pay plan for warehouse employees we installed. Small-team (pickers, packers, drivers, etc.), performance pay was indexed to the overall warehouse controllable net income. Three months into the program I was invited back to talk to various employees about the program. My first meeting was with three of the supervisors. Early on, it was clear these supervisors were angry about the performance pay system. I asked why and they replied, "Corporate just bought a new office building next door. We have to uncrate the furniture they purchased for the building. I can tell you, they have expensive taste! These pricey furnishings are killing our gainshare opportunity."

The warehouse controllable net income was:

revenue - (payroll + returns + freight)

Furnishings were not in this number. This was the first time these supervisors had actually seen the expense elements that made up the warehouse CNI. Further discussion revealed that the employees in the warehouse were trying to reduce labor expense through fewer part-time hours and reduced overtime. However, the effect on the CNI had been negligible.

A review of the line item expenses in the CNI revealed that freight expense was some 70 percent of the total controllable expenses. The supervisors quickly saw they had been working on the wrong expense category and decided to meet again to develop a plan to reduce freight expenses. Empowerment means sharing information!

Some years ago, I was orienting a group of bank item processing employees in Hawaii to their performance pay system. I explained that the performance pay opportunity would be determined by improvements in the ratio of payroll and "float" expense to the number of items processed. The operators stared at me with blank looks. One of them finally asked me, "What is float?"

I was surprised at the question since float is a major expense for a bank and is controlled, in large part, by these employees. I explained that when a customer cashes a check on a bank from a second bank, the first bank has essentially "loaned" the customer the money until the bank receives its payment from the customer's bank. These funds are unavailable to the first bank as long as they are outstanding and that bank must borrow the funds to cover its customer's loans. Similarly, the slower a deposit is processed, the longer it is unavailable to the bank. A one-day delay in processing could amount to thousands of dollars in interest expense to the first bank.

The employees looked at each other. Finally, one of them said, "We thought the bank wanted these checks processed quickly just to reduce overtime! Now that we understand what float is, it seems to us that it would make sense to process the high-dollar checks written on other banks first." I agreed. "Then our courier pickups are routed all wrong! The high-dollar items are, in many cases, picked up last and we can't get them processed in time to receive same-day credit."

The employees spent the remainder of the meeting developing new courier routes. The result was that their performance pay pool was totally funded before one item was processed. Employees can improve the profits of an organization only when they understand how it operates, and will only when they have a personal stake in the improvement.

Indexing pay to organizational profitability aligns employee and management goals. Expense savings go directly into the employee's paycheck as do increases in revenue. In another bank installation, I learned that the power of profit-pay indexing can work against an organization if designed incorrectly.

We installed a performance pay system in a bank's sixty branches. Each employee's personal performance pay was indexed to the "controllable net income" of the branch. About six months into the program I received a call from the bank. One of the branches was robbed a few months prior and during the robbery some of the windows were shot out. The branch employees elected not to replace the windows to avoid the expense. In itself, this was admirable, but it was snowing on customers!

Will employees get-cost sensitive when they share in cost savings? You bet! These employees, however, were

23

obviously shortsighted (as are many managers and owners). We explained to them that lost revenue was difficult to recover and that this lack of service would ultimately hurt them more than the modest savings they were getting from not replacing the windows. An alternative would have been to remove repair expense from the "controllable net income."

Treating Employees as Owners Instead of Commodities. Conventional pay treats employees as commodities that have an exchange value like a loaf of bread or a gallon of gasoline. An employee's education, skills, and experience are compared to a market value to determine the salary or wage. In contrast, the pay of an owner or self-employed person is determined by the profitability of their business. The more profitable the business, the more the owner earns. There is no average salary or pay norm for owners.

When an organization makes the transition from conventional wages and salaries to profit-indexed pay, employees will be paid more like owners. Their education and experience no longer guarantee a market salary. On the other hand, their pay is also no longer limited by their market value. In a profit-indexed pay system, employees with little education or experience can earn much more than in the conventional system if they perform well and their company is successful.

References

1) Martin Weitzman. *The Share Economy.* Cambridge, MA: Harvard University Press, 1984.

Chapter 3: Pay for Time

MANY MANAGERS ARE CONFUSED ABOUT PRODUCTIVITY, ITS RELA-
TIONSHIP TO CUSTOMER SERVICE, AND HOW TO IMPROVE IT. A CASE IS
MADE FOR MAKING PRODUCTIVITY IMPROVEMENTS A DIRECT BENEFIT
TO WORKERS TO ENCOURAGE OPTIMAL PERFORMANCE.

What is Productivity? Productivity is the relationship of output to input. Output is the quantity of goods and services produced or the revenue generated by those goods and services. Labor input is the labor hours or labor expense associated with producing the output. Productivity only improves when either output increases or input decreases. For example, a company's monthly revenue is $100,000 while its payroll is $50,000. The expense/revenue ratio is $50,000 / $100,000 or 50%. We can improve the expense ratio by either lowering payroll or increasing revenue. A $10,000 increase in revenue, with no additional hires, would yield an expense ratio of $50,000/$110,000 = 45%.

A common mistake is to equate efficiency with productivity. If employees work faster because of better training, motivation or technology, we assume productivity has improved. But has it? I consulted with a bank several years ago to help improve its productivity in the item processing area. The operators were processing an average 1,100 items an hour when we began. We installed a performance feedback system that enabled each operator to compute their item processing rate at the end of the day. Over a few weeks, the average rate rose to 1700 items an hour (with a lower error rate). We then added a performance pay plan in which operators could earn an additional five percent of base pay for meeting daily item

25

rate goals. The average processing rate rose again to 2,300 items per hour (over a 100 percent improvement).

2.3 Management was quite excited with this improvement until they received their monthly financial reports. The labor cost per item had not been reduced. Despite the 100 percent increase in operator efficiency, the item processing manager had not reduced staff or operator hours. Therefore, the labor cost per item did not improve. In fact, the performance pay somewhat increased the cost per item.

There were, however, benefits to the bank in the improved operator efficiency. The 100 percent increase in processing efficiency allowed the bank to meet earlier sending deadlines and thereby reduce "float" or interest expense on the items. Reducing this expense was a much higher savings than could have been obtained by reducing the operator payroll. Still, we had not improved productivity.

To solve this problem, we designed a supervisor performance pay plan. This plan rewarded the supervisors for improving operator "utilization." Utilization is the ratio of time in production to time-sheet hours. The supervisor can improve utilization by reducing operator hours or increasing time in production. A few months into the program, the supervisors were complaining that the more efficient their employees became, the less performance pay the supervisors earned!

A review of the operator and supervisor performance pay plans found this to be true. When operator efficiency improved, on a constant work volume, the operator time in production declined. The faster you go, the quicker you get done. This inverse relationship was embarrassingly obvious to us as soon as we thought about it. The following example is based on twenty operators working an eight-hour day.

Relationships among Efficiency, Utilization and Productivity.

Efficiency = items/production hours

Utilization = production hours/time sheet hours

Productivity = items/time sheet hours

	Wage-based Operator Efficiency	Incentive-based Operator Efficiency
Items per day	132,000	132,000
Production hours	120	57
Items per prod. hr.	1,100	2,300
(efficiency increase)		
	Utilization	Utilization
Production hours	120	57
Time sheet hours	160	160
Utilization percent	75%	36%
(utilization decrease)		
	Productivity	Productivity
Items per day	132,000	132,000
Time sheet hours	160	160
Items per hour	825	825
(no change)		

3.5

These relationships among efficiency, utilization, and productivity are widely misunderstood. You simply can't achieve a productivity improvement without either increasing work volume or reducing staff. Productivity improvements are always obtained by either not adding staff when volumes increase, or reducing staff when work volumes remain constant.

We had completed the design of performance pay plans for all the employees in a company except for two elderly ladies who had been with the organization for many years. The owner was very concerned about how well they would adapt to performance measurement and pay.

Several weeks after the plan was implemented, we met with the two employees to see how they liked it. "We think it's interesting but can't understand why you want to pay us extra money when we meet the goal. There isn't enough work for both of us to hit the daily goal, so I do all the work on Monday and Betty does it on Tuesday and so on!" Efficiency improvements are of little benefit without a strategy for utilizing the freed-up time.

How Does Productivity Affect Service Quality? On the other hand, it is a "shell game" to believe that productivity improvement is nothing more than reducing staff. Many organizations and many productivity consulting firms simply lay off employees to improve productivity. This "downsizing" strategy tacitly assumes either that the turnaround time of the product or service is unimportant, or that employee efficiency will automatically improve as staff is reduced.

3.6

In my experiences with companies who had previously reduced their staffing, I found they often believed that

28

employee efficiency would automatically improve as staff size was reduced. Employees would become more efficient simply because they had to. In one company, the time required to process an application had increased from seven days to twenty-seven days after a staff reduction. Apparently the employees weren't aware of the automatic increase in efficiency resulting from downsizing.

Another viewpoint is that even if layoffs do increase product and service turnaround time, that's not as important an issue as reducing labor costs. If it doesn't make any difference how timely a product or service is, then the company doesn't need *any* staff since it makes no difference whether the work gets done at all.

It seems that the reason so many organizations lay off employees, without regard to the adverse impact on service or product timeliness, is largely due to the failure of most organizations to measure timeliness consistently and treat it as a "line item" on their income statement. Further, labor expense reductions immediately improve the bottom line while the effects of declining timeliness are more ambiguous and delayed (though often much more costly than the labor savings). The following formula describes the relationship between timeliness and employee productivity (for simplicity, all formulas assume a constant volume).

(Work Volume/Productivity)/Hours=Turnaround Time

For example, if 1,000 units are processed, and the average staff productivity is 10 units per hour, given 80 staff hours a day the turnaround time will be:

(1,000/10 = 100)/80=1.25 days turnaround time

If, to improve productivity, we cut the staff hours to sixty a day but don't improve employee efficiency, the turnaround time will be:

(1,000/10 = 100)/60=1.67 days turnaround time

To maintain our service requirement turnaround time of 1.25 days we would need to improve employee productivity from 10 units per hour to 13.33 units per hour.

(1,000/13.33 = 75)/60=1.25 days turnaround time

The following two formulas summarize the relationships among turnaround time, productivity and efficiency.

Turnaround time = (Work Volume/Productivity)/Hours

Productivity = Efficiency x Utilization

Given these relationships, clearly a reduction in staff hours without an improvement in efficiency will increase turnaround time. It is also clear that a customer service improvement based on quicker turnaround will require an efficiency improvement unless there is an increase in staff hours (quality is not free). Considering the second formula, we can improve productivity without damaging service only by increasing employee efficiency or utilization. Employees must either process work faster, or spend more of the day in production. *Neither of these improvements can be achieved by simply downsizing. Both require employee cooperation.*

What Is Preventing High Productivity? In one company I worked with we, were considering using "time off" as an incentive rather than cash. We met with all the employees in the department and announced that as soon as all the department's work was completed, all employees could go home

30

and still receive a full day's pay. The next day, and for most days thereafter, the department closed down by noon! Clearly there was a 50 percent productivity improvement opportunity that wasn't being realized.

It is important to note that productivity did not decline just because everyone went home at noon. The labor cost per unit remained the same. But the turnaround time was cut in half. Customer work was completed by noon instead of five. We gained a service improvement though no productivity improvement.

If you want to find out what the productivity improvement opportunity is in an area of your company, simply allow employees to go home at full pay when the work is completed. I have performed this experiment many times and consistently find significant productivity improvement opportunities.

It is the conventional wage system that constrains employee productivity. "When you pay for time, you get time." You get what you pay for. The wage system focuses on time. Time is an expense, not a result. Because we fail to measure job results, we manage time. We supervise showing up on time, break time, and absenteeism. It's like saying, "I don't care what you accomplish, just be here!" This emphasis on time destroys productivity. Employees learn to look busy to prevent a cutback of hours or jobs. Worse, they may extend time to earn overtime pay. But, "busyness isn't business." The hourly wage pay system is responsible for the focus on time rather than results because it pays for time rather than results.

Imagine you spend a Saturday afternoon mowing your yard. When you are finished, you run breathlessly into the house and announce to your family that you have made a real improvement in your mowing efforts. It used to take you two hours to mow the yard, but you have figured out how to do it in four! This is the illogic of time-based pay. The longer it takes to complete the task, the more money you make.

Time-based pay isn't natural. It isn't the way people manage their own lives. The result of time-based management is to restrain the natural desire of the individual to become more efficient; to find better ways to do things. When the employee is, in effect, punished for applying timesaving skills, one can only guess at the effects of this unnatural state of affairs on employee morale and initiative.

Supervisors who have long experience in managing time may actually discourage productivity and service quality improvements. Over and over we have installed performance pay systems to find supervisors working against the program. If an employee finishes early, the supervisor criticizes him for having nothing to do or gives him extra work assignments. Managing time is a hard habit to break.

Of course, if we encourage our supervisor to stop managing time and undermining employee productivity, we must provide them something else to manage. That something is results. We must provide the supervisor objective performance results by which to manage. We must replace time on a job with measures of departmental, team, and personal productivity, timeliness, and accuracy.

How Do You Improve Productivity? The key organizational change that must occur to create a high-productivity organization is to make productivity improvement a benefit for employees. The success of any improvement strategy —

be it management training, skills training, reengineering, process improvements, group problem-solving, self-directed work teams, TQM, or others — is to ensure that the improvement benefits the employee. If productivity improvements have a negative impact on employees, no amount of training or exhortation will work.

The conventional pay system is antithetical to productivity improvement. Since it pays for time, and productivity is the reduction of time, conventional pay cannot support a productivity improvement effort. It is the worst kind of hypocrisy to ask employees to develop productivity improvement plans when the ultimate outcome will be to reduce that same employee's pay through staff reductions or cutbacks in hours and overtime. Bluntly, we are asking employees to "please find a way to cut your pay!"

The solution to this problem is relatively simple — share productivity savings with employees. The policy will be, "If our work volume increases, and you can meet our service levels without additional staff, we will share these savings with you. If an employee leaves and you can handle that employee's work load without a decline in quality, we will share that employee's pay with you. If your team cross-trains and loans out employees to other areas, we will pay you for it. Or if some of your team members move to flex-time, we will pay you for it."

How long should you share a productivity improvement with employees? Forever. Productivity is dynamic. You must continue sharing to maintain the improvement. One-time payment, suggestion systems and the like miss the point. Employees must benefit on an ongoing basis. As an analogy, when do you stop paying wages and salaries?

How much of the savings should you share? I suggest that in service industries, you compute your payroll to revenue percentage and share that percentage. In manufacturing, compute the payroll as a percentage of gross profit. For example, if your annual payroll was $400,000 and your annual revenue was $1,000,000, your payroll percentage of revenue would be 40 percent. You would share 40 percent of each payroll dollar saved, with employees. If you further qualify profit sharing with performance measures, you may wish to consider sharing more than the 40 percent, since many employees will not attain goal performance on their performance measures.

This approach to productivity improvement is termed "gainsharing." Gainsharing plans such as *Scanlon* and *Improshare* have been with us for many years. Research on these programs finds many of them have been effective at reducing payroll expense (and other expenses). The *Profit-Indexed Performance Pay* approach will be outlined in later chapters. This approach is a significant departure from traditional gainshare programs in that it indexes payouts to company profitability and qualifies payouts based upon performance at the team or personal level.

Whatever approach to gainsharing you choose, it should address the components of productivity improvement described earlier in this chapter. That is, it should encourage employees to improve efficiency and utilization without sacrificing quality and responsiveness. To prevent a degradation in turnaround time, you must "qualify" or adjust the employee savings share by the percentage of the turnaround goal that is achieved.

To foster employee efficiency improvements, you should install a non-competitive, team-based, performance pay system that provides a personal benefit to high-efficiency employees for sharing their skills with others. Productivity improvement based upon simply working harder has a rather low ceiling. You should encourage your employees to meet in teams and develop process improvements. In other words "Work smarter — not harder." Productivity improvements that involve capital expenditures should be added to the cost per unit on a prorated or depreciation basis; employees should share the cost of capital improvements, as well as the benefits.

There are many proven strategies for improving employee utilization. These include job reengineering, work scheduling, work distribution, work flow improvement, and cross-utilization. Managers and supervisors should be trained in these techniques. Organizations with self-directed work teams should train teams in these techniques.

I am generally opposed to skills-based pay where base pay increases are awarded to employees who expand their skill sets. My experience with these programs is that they can significantly increase fixed payroll expense and may do little to ensure that the new skills are applied in other job positions.

I have had good success, however, with a variant of skills-based pay we term "team franchising." One-time payments are made for learning other jobs. Team members are paid incentives based upon the productivity of the team. The team can increase its productivity by "loaning" employees to other teams. These loaned hours are subtracted from the loaning team's productivity ratio and added as borrowed hours to the borrowing team's productivity ratio. The borrowing team benefits by being able to meet work load deadlines without adding full-time staff. To loan employees to other teams, the team members must become cross-trained in the other teams' job functions. The performance payment is awarded for doing the work — not learning the work.

In some cases, added skills are of value to an organization even though the skills are not applied each month. In these instances, the employee performance pay *basis* can be increased to reward the attainment of new skills. The basis is discussed in Section II. Essentially, an increase in an employee's performance pay basis increases the employee's performance pay opportunity.

Chapter 4: Corporate Socialism

THREE TYPES OF PAY EQUITY ARE DISCUSSED: EQUITY ACROSS OR-GANIZATIONS, EQUITY WITHIN AN ORGANIZATION, AND EQUITY OF OP-PORTUNITY. THE CONVENTIONAL PAY SYSTEM ADDRESSES ONLY THE INTER-ORGANIZATIONAL EQUITY ISSUE.

We are social creatures. The fairness of the workplace is as important to us as how much we are paid. I have been in organizations where a person earning $100,000 is angry because the person next door earns $110,000. For any pay system to be effective, it must deal with three equity issues: pay equity between the company and other organizations (market pay), pay equity across employees within the organization, and pay equity with respect to performance pay opportunity and personal effort.

Pay Equity Across Organizations. Employees are concerned about whether their pay is comparable to that of other organizations. Most organizations attempt to provide pay that is comparable to other companies in their area. This is accomplished informally by reviewing the want ads and calling other companies. Pay surveys are also available that list pay statistics for various job groups in different regions.

When an organization installs a performance-based pay system, the issues change. One company I worked with implemented a pay freeze for three years. The company's job marketplace had an average five percent increase during each of the three years. At the end of the three-year freeze, the company's employees were paid fifteen percent less than the average base pay across the job market. Concurrent with the freeze, employee performance pay opportunities were increased ten percent a year.

This increase in performance pay opportunity averaged ten percent a year or two times the base pay increases that were frozen. Employees who achieved one hundred percent of their performance pay goals could earn up to an additional thirty percent above the original base pay by the end of the three-year period (if the company profits were sufficient). This thirty percent of base pay earnings meant these employees could earn back the fifteen percent pay lost in the freeze plus fifteen percent above what they would have made.

The following table describes the effects of this procedure on a high-, average-, and low-performing employee who each earned ten dollars an hour before the pay freeze.

	Initial Hourly Pay	Hourly Pay After 3 Years	Total Pay With Incentive*
Market Pay	$10.00	$11.50	$11.50
High Performer	$10.00	$10.00	$13.00
Avg. Performer	$10.00	$10.00	$11.50
Low Performer	$10.00	$10.00	$10.00

* effects of compounding excluded for simplicity

4.1A

The company found it difficult to hire new employees when they let the base pay fall more than fifteen percent below market. They therefore reinstituted the annual market-comparable base pay increases after three years. Because of the three years' pay freeze, however, their guaranteed pay remained fifteen percent below market.

The freeze was designed to better reward high performers. Assuming a normal distribution of high and low performers in the company, the total payroll cost increase to the company was a net of zero, since each base pay increase dollar that was not paid to low performers was paid in incentives to high performers. The procedure was a redistribution of pay, not a payroll reduction. Had all employees become high performers, the profits of the organization would increase, enabling all employees to earn above-market pay.

Besides paying high performers more than low performers, the freeze yielded two additional benefits to the company. Turnover in the top quartile of performers decreased significantly, though, interestingly, it decreased across all levels of performers. Perhaps the opportunity to earn above-market pay, rather than the actual earnings, was the cause.

A second benefit was realized in the company's hiring process. Individuals applying for a position in the company were informed that the guaranteed pay was fifteen percent below market. High performers, though, could earn fifteen percent above market if the organization was successful. It was management's opinion that employees who chose not to work under this arrangement were no serious loss to the company. The performance pay system enabled the company to recruit high performers and discourage low performers from applying.

Pay Equity Within the Organization. The entitlement pay system bases pay on the job position rather than on the performance of the person in the job. The worth of a job is graded using a point system or survey of what other companies pay for the same or similar jobs. The value of the employee's performance is then rewarded by advancement through several wage or salary grades or through annual increases to base pay.

Survey research finds that this system provides only small pay differentials among employees in the same job position. The typical percentage difference between an exceptional performer and a mediocre one averages only six to ten percent nationwide. For a $25,000-a-year job, this amounts to only an average $35 a week additional pay to the high achiever. The actual percentage difference in the value of work produced by a high achiever compared with a mediocre performer, however, runs 30 percent to 300 percent depending upon the control the employee has over the job results. Comparing differences in pay to differences in the value of work produced, the inequities range from a 4:1 ratio to a 100:1 ratio.

As an illustration of this type of inequity, let's assume two chemists are employed in a job in which the average salary is $30,000 a year. The exceptional chemist completes 1,000 tests a year and the average chemist 750 tests a year. The exceptional chemist's salary is $32,000 a year, while the average chemist earns $30,000. The exceptional chemist is paid about 6.5 percent more than the average chemist.

We are paying the average chemist $30,000 to produce 750 tests or $40 per test. But we pay the exceptional chemist $32,000 to produce 1,000 tests or $32 per test. In reality, relative to the tests produced, we are paying the exceptional chemist much *less* than the average chemist. If we adjusted the average chemist's pay for what she would earn at the same level of production as the exceptional chemist, we would be paying $40 X 1,000 tests = $40,000 to produce an equivalent number of tests. Per test produced, the average chemist effectively should earn $8,000 more per year than the exceptional chemist.

It is clear the entitlement pay system does a poor job of rewarding the exceptional performer. Why do organizations allow this inequity to exist? One reason is that most organizations do not *objectively* measure employee performance. Instead, each employee's immediate supervisor *subjectively* "evaluates" the employee's performance once a year. In other words, one reason we don't pay people what they're worth is we don't *know* what they're worth.

Another, more insidious reason for this inequity is the socialistic philosophy of entitlement thinking that has developed in many organizations. This view says that employees in the same job should earn about the same pay — regardless of their performance. As Karl Marx said, "From each according to his ability — to each according to his need."

Entitlement pay is a politics of envy. The mediocre employee is envious of the exceptional performer's ability or motivation to achieve. A communist proverb was "If your neighbor has two cows and you have one, kill one of his." To maintain harmony, management chooses to ignore differences in the value of contributions among employees. The result is a pay system that is unfair to achievers.

In contrast, a performance pay system pays for work accomplished. In our previous example, the average cost of a test was ($30,000 + $32,000)/(750 tests + 1,000 tests) = $35.40 per test. If we paid this fee per test completed, the two chemists' earnings would be:

41

Average Chemist = $35.40 x 750 = $26,550

Exceptional Chemist = $35.40 x 1,000 = $35,400

The total compensation expense to the organization remains the same. The pay is simply redistributed to pay the exceptional performer more than the conventional salary system paid. Is this redistribution a good idea? Well, if we pay employees the same, regardless of their personal contributions, we are unfair to our best people. On the other hand, if we pay based on actual performance, we risk irritating our poor performers. The simple question is, whom do we want to avoid irritating — good or poor performers?

Equity of Opportunity. A curious notion that pervades the entitlement culture is that results should always equal effort. Trying hard is more important than success. "It's not who wins or loses — but how the game is played" that's important. This idea has a nice sound to it, but creates severe problems in the real world of business. We have come to accept the idea that if we simply try hard, we shouldn't also be required to be effective.

Working hard at the wrong things is not of value to an organization, or for that matter, to a society. The free market, absent government intervention, doesn't reward people who produce things no one wants to buy. Neither should a company. Would you really want to fly with a pilot who tries very hard but can't seem to fly a plane? We have confused effort with results. On a professional golf tour there is a very small difference in the effort or skill of the best golfer and the field. However, it is that difference that wins the tournament. Hard work is not important — results are!

The critical flaw with the notion that effort is what's important is that employees are not aligned with the organization's objectives and, therefore, performance does not improve. I have been in dozens of companies where work procedures are never upgraded. Employees simply follow by rote whatever they are told to do. "We've always done it this way." Their objective is to fill up eight hours, not to produce anything. Time-based pay schemes like wages and salaries exacerbate this problem. They reward low productivity.

Entitlement thinking is so ingrained in employee thinking that employees demand performance pay even when the job isn't completed. "I tried hard; I did everything you asked; it's not my fault" are common excuses of employees newly introduced to pay for performance. I often counter with an example. Imagine a commissioned salesperson made a sales call. He dressed correctly, took all the right materials, showed up on time, and made the sales presentation exactly as trained. The prospect still didn't buy. The salesperson then returns to the sales manager and demands the sales commission. "I did everything you asked and really tried hard. Even though I didn't sell anything — I deserve the commission." What do you think the sales manager's response would be? Yet this is exactly the reaction we receive from many employees who have been living in the entitlement culture.

When I am designing performance pay plans for an organization, the client often wants to make adjustments to goals based on work or resource availability. "We are a seasonal business. Therefore our performance pay goals should vary with the season. We should expect fewer sales during the off- season and a lot of sales during the peak season. After all, it's not the employee's fault that no one buys during the slack season." No, it isn't — but it isn't the company's fault either. Why should the employee be sheltered from the business cycles of the organization? Why not simply pay them a lot when they sell and pay less when they don't?

A well-designed performance pay system provides employees *equity of opportunity — but not necessarily equity of result.* Equity of opportunity is ensured in three ways. First, employee performance measures should relate to outcomes employees can strongly influence. This requirement means the measurement should be made as close to the individual employee as is practical. Organization-wide profit-sharing fails this criterion. The measure is taken too far away from the influence of most individuals within the organization.

Second, performance payouts should be made for incremental improvement over current performance. National norms and "benchmarking" should be avoided in the design of performance pay plans. If you are self-employed, incremental improvement earns you more, regardless of how your performance compares to others. Further, performance goals should be established to achieve organizational results — not simply to increase performance. The sad history of performance pay at the beginning of this century is largely due to management increasing goals each year whether business objectives required an increase or not. Constantly increasing performance goals is equivalent to continual, base-pay reductions in a conventional entitlement pay system. When goals are increased, the pay opportunity should be increased concurrently.

Third, employees must be ultimately "empowered" to allow them to capitalize on the performance pay opportunity. Management cannot arbitrarily assign employees other duties that interfere with their performance pay earnings opportunity. New accountabilities must be added to the performance pay plan. This addition should be adjusted for by an increase in performance pay earnings opportunity, a removal of other accountabilities from the plan, or a reduction in other accountabilities' goals. Employees should also be enabled to make decisions and change processes that directly affect their performance pay earnings opportunity. Employees who are going to be paid as if self-employed must also be self-managed.

Chapter 5: Competition and Cooperation

MANAGEMENT PRACTICES THAT FOSTER COMPETITION AMONG EM-
PLOYEES WHO NEED TO COOPERATE SHOULD BE AVOIDED. CONVEN-
TIONAL PAY SYSTEMS OFTEN RELY ON PROMOTIONS AS REWARDS FOR
GOOD PERFORMANCE. THIS PRACTICE CREATES A TOP-HEAVY ORGANI-
ZATION AND EMPLOYEE COMPETITION.

It is common wisdom in this country that competition is the source of success. Competition among people is encouraged from preschool games through adulthood. Winners and losers have been an integral part of our culture. Capitalism is also a competition among businesses and has been shown to be the most effective economic system. It would follow, then, that competition among employees in an organization would also prove beneficial. But this assumption has proven to be a false one.

Problems with competition. Our early attempts at designing employee performance pay systems were organized around competition. We created programs that rewarded the best performer in the group. Over time, we found these programs achieved modest success, at best, and often actually decreased total group performance. The explanation has since become evident.

Two factors operate to make competitive performance pay plans unlikely to improve an employee group's performance. In any group there is typically a top performer. The reasons are various. The employee has more job experience, natural aptitudes, or is more competitive due to past successes. A program that rewards the best performer will begin by rewarding this individual exclusively.

In time, the rest of the group will often give up. The program will thus have little effect on the majority of the employees. The performance pay or recognition will affect the top performer but, by definition, the results will be minimal since her performance was already exceptional. For a competitive system to work well, everyone in the group would have to start and remain at about the same level of performance.

The second factor that limits the utility of competitive programs is that most work groups are also social groups. Winning at the expense of others damages the social relationships within the group. In one case, the top performer, and consistent winner, in one of our early competitive systems, came to me privately and asked that the system be removed. He had become an outcast in the employee group for always winning. But, he enjoyed working at a high level of proficiency. Our competitive system *was forcing him to work below his abilities.*

The solution: Compete against goals. Competition doesn't have to be directed against others. We can compete with ourselves. We can strive to achieve a goal or to improve over past performance. The sports analogy is found in golf, where you play against par rather than against someone else. Performance pay plans can provide this sort of competition within the workplace and avoid the pitfalls of competition among employees. The employee works against goal, or for improvement, not against other employees.

Never implement a competition among employees who must cooperate to get the job done!

47

Conventional Pay and the "Peter Principle." The Peter Principle states "Employees rise to their level of incompetence." Employees are promoted until they reach a position in which they perform poorly and from which they cannot be promoted. Most of us find Dr. Peter's observation accurate for many people. What is less clear, though, is why management engages in this practice. Again, we should look for the reason in the conventional pay system.

Conventional pay severely restricts supervisor and manager access to employee pay as a reward strategy for high performance. The supervisor cannot immediately reward exceptional performance through pay — except once a year through the performance appraisal and merit increase process. Further, there are typically restrictions on how much of a pay increase can be awarded. Some companies even require a forced distribution in which the supervisor must "rob Peter to pay Paul." Each significant pay increase must be balanced with an offsetting lower increase for some other employee. This practice creates a "zero sum game" in which some employees can benefit only if others suffer.

Another feature of conventional pay is the application of fixed pay bands, or ranges, to each job position. When an employee reaches the top of his job's pay range, there is no means provided for additional pay opportunities except to move to a better paying position. These pay practices severely hamper the use of pay as a reward for exceptional performance. Consequently, the supervisor must look for other ways to reward outstanding employees.

A common reward technique is to promote the good performer to management. The problem with using promotions

48

as rewards is that we are constantly moving the best performers in a job position out of the job and into management. This practice necessarily lowers overall performance in each job position. Even after training, the replacement will most likely perform as an average performer, not an exceptional one. "Fast-track" employees may also show little commitment to the job-of-the-moment (and in some cases little commitment to customers) and simply see the position as a stepping stone to management.

A second problem with using promotions as rewards is that we not only lose the best performer in a job, we may also create a dissatisfied and ineffective manager. This happens because the correlation between high performance and success as a manager may be low or even negative. High performance in the job may predict poor management rather than good management.

I was asked to design a sales performance pay plan in one organization. Before we began the design sessions, I was told that the manager was new. He had been the best salesman, and was therefore selected to replace the previous manager when he left. The first few days I was in the department, I found it very difficult to meet with the sales manager as he was always out of the office. On the other hand, the salespeople appeared to have a lot of time on their hands and spent much of it in the office socializing.

Over time, I discovered that the sales manager was attempting to meet his department's sales goals by increasing his own sales enough to cover all six salespeople — and he was almost doing it! The new sales manager knew how to sell and liked selling, but had no idea, and little interest in how to manage others. The company had lost its best salesman and created a dissatisfied, ineffective sales manager. The likelihood of a good performer becoming a good manager appears to be inversely related to how much independent action the original job required. Jobs where the employee works mostly alone, and with little supervision, seem most likely to produce poor managers.

A third problem with using promotions as rewards is that it is a competitive pay system that pits employees against each other for a limited number of management positions. Competition for promotion among employees may work well in situations where the employees are not required to work as a team. But in areas where cooperation and mutual support are important, using promotions as rewards can substantially reduce the productivity and morale of the area.

Finally, promotions as rewards put pressure on the organization to create more and more management positions to reward exceptional performers. This pressure creates an ever-expanding bureaucracy that is expensive and makes the organization less flexible and less responsive to change.

For example, banks have been notorious for promoting people rather than paying them. As a result, there are numerous assistant vice presidents, vice presidents, senior vice presidents, executive vice presidents, and, in one bank, senior executive vice president. In meetings with bank management we have said this practice wouldn't be so bad if only employees wouldn't take the title seriously and try to manage someone!

Flat vs. Tall Organizations. Conventional pay fosters excessive layers of management by using promotions as rewards. This is not, however, the only way that conventional

pay creates bureaucracy — there are at least two other factors. First, a business culture has developed in which it is
"up or out." People who remain producers rather than moving into management are seen as failures.

When the Soviet Union was beginning its transformation
from socialism to a market economy, I met with some Soviet
trade representatives. In our discussions they told me that in
the Soviet Union under communism, managers were seen as
inferior to workers. Becoming a manager was, effectively, a
demotion. I point this out only to demonstrate that there is
no inherent connection between ability and a person's choice
to either be a worker, or to manage and work through others.
This bias toward management is expensive and greatly con-
tributes to highly bureaucratic organizational structures.

A second way that conventional pay encourages bureaucracy
is the hierarchical, "command and control" management
structure required to manage large numbers of employees
who are paid for time rather than results. The basic management structure of most organizations in not very different
from the principles of management laid down by Moses and
the Hebrew tribes thousands of years ago. A manager's
"span of control" was determined by how many people he
could talk to on a day-to-day basis. Henri Fayol, the management theorist, stated the ideal span of control in a hierarchy
was seven.

In a company of 200 employees this requires:

200 employees/7 = 29 managers who must then be managed
by 4 other managers who then report to the chief executive
(34 managers in total). Contrast this with Lincoln Electric in
Cleveland, Ohio, whose 2,500 employees are paid entirely on

51

piece-rate and profit sharing. Lincoln Electric's management span of control is reported to be an average 100 employees per manager — a span of control of 100:1 rather than 7:1.

Flat

5,4

Managing Without Managers. How does performance pay allow an organization to increase its management span of control and create a flatter organizational structure? The two reasons seem, at first, to be paradoxical. One is improved communications and control through the implementation of precision, performance measurement.

The other is a reduction in the need to directly supervise employees when they are paid for measurable results rather than the time spent doing a job. One provides management more control; the other provides employees more control. Both objectives are achieved through installing a performance pay system. As an example, how much direct supervision do salespeople on straight commission require?

A performance pay system replaces direct supervision with objective, performance measurement. Ancient military leaders had to talk to their subordinates, who then had to talk to their subordinates, and so on to direct performance, and determine whether their orders were being carried out. Performance pay plans that track the performance of small teams or individual employees, direct performance and monitor whether goals are being accomplished, thus substantially reducing the need for personal communications up and down the line. Performance pay plans substantially reduce the need for layers of middle management. Senior management can direct large groups of employees through changes in performance pay measures, priority weights and goals.

Why don't employees cooperate? Many business people worry that performance pay will decrease cooperation among employees and ultimately overall productivity and service. The question that should be asked is "Do wages and salaries foster cooperation?" Annual increases and promotions are based on the individual employee's performance appraisal, not the team's. Forced pay increase distributions are required in the budgeting process. This means that if someone receives a high increase, someone else must necessarily receive a low one.

When promotions are used to reward outstanding performance, it is also necessarily a zero sum game in which employees must compete for limited advancement opportunities. It is difficult to comprehend how conventional pay promotes cooperation, but easy to see how it creates competition. In my work with clients, a common situation is that everyone seems to dislike the salespeople. The credit and collections departments complain that the salespeople sell things to people who don't pay and that they fail to complete the credit forms correctly. The operations and customer service groups complain that the salespeople make promises they can't keep to customers and fail to specify the product accurately.

Though there is maybe some truth to these complaints, a more basic reason for this antagonism is found again in the pay system. Most organizations provide their sales force some sort of sales commissions. The more the salesperson sells, the more he earns. In contrast, other support employees usually don't participate in the commissions. The more the salespeople sell, the more work the support people must do for the same pay. No wonder there is antagonism! Companies that install commission plans, in which a limited number of employees can participate, are bound to create pay inequities. The solution to the sales problem is simply to include the support groups in the performance pay system.

Finally, companies should never install contest-type incentive plans. Putting people in competition who must cooperate with each other on a daily basis is counterproductive. So much so, that we recommend eliminating "employee of the month" programs when they create a competitive environment. Competition should be against goal — not each other. The proper type of competition in an organization would be more similar to golf or bowling where you compete against par or shoot for 300. Well-meaning performance pay systems can be poorly designed, and competitive systems are one example.

Chapter 6: Management by Perception

MANAGEMENT BY PERCEPTION REFERS TO THE COMMON PRACTICE OF ANNUAL EMPLOYEE PERFORMANCE APPRAISALS THAT ARE BASED UPON THE SUPERVISOR'S SUBJECTIVE IMPRESSIONS OF THE EMPLOYEE RATHER THAN OBJECTIVE DATA. THIS PRACTICE POLITICIZES THE WORKPLACE, DISCOURAGES GOOD LEADERSHIP, AND PREVENTS EMPLOYEE EMPOWERMENT.

Management by Perception refers to the practice of subjective performance reviews for merit pay and promotions that is common in the conventional pay system. This practice is harmful to the organization in three ways. First, it fails to align employee goals with the business goals of the organization by creating a political rather than a business environment. Second, it allows managers to avoid the difficult task of objectively specifying and tracking true job outcomes. And third, it prevents employee "empowerment" since the employee's fate is tied to supervisor opinion rather than actual performance.

The Politics of Management by Perception. In a restaurant chain, my first assignment was to improve the sales performance of cocktail servers. The first thing I did when I arrived, was to ask the three restaurant managers to rank the five cocktail servers in terms of wine and liquor sales. After I collected the guest checks for the previous two weeks and totaled the actual sales for each server, we then compared the manager rankings with the actual sales.

One server sold thirty percent more per hour than any of the others. To my surprise, she was ranked as the lowest performer by the managers. Further, all three managers ranked another server as the best performer, but her actual sales were only average. What was going on?

The key factor was how well the employees got along with the managers. This factor is a general issue across all types of companies. The best performer, who had been ranked lowest, was on probation. This employee did not get along well with management but got along quite well with customers. She argued with managers and generally did not respond well to management directives. I have no scientific evidence, but suspect that top performers are often independent sorts who find it difficult to be subservient to management. It really isn't surprising that management ranked employees according to who was easiest to deal with and whom they liked in the absence of objective data. (It's worth noting, however, that once they learned how much the server on probation sold, she was removed from probation.)

Not having objective data, we rely on subjective perceptions to evaluate people. These perceptions are complex and inevitably colored by social variables that may have little to do with job performance. Of course we would prefer to reward people we like, but this isn't always good business. The conventional pay system, with its annual subjective reviews, substitutes supervisor perceptions for actual employee performance results. This practice "politicizes" the workplace. The cynical view "it's not what you know, but whom you know" accurately reflects the reality of this situation.

When internal politics are more important than results in determining an employee's success, an inward focus develops that is ultimately injurious to the organization's ability to satisfy its customers and compete with other organizations. I personally believe the recent emphasis on "internal customers" adds to this problem. A performance pay system can reorient the focus of an employee group from internal politics to external business reality by defining and paying on key results that impact true business outcomes.

6.3 Positive Leadership. We should train managers in how to state performance goals objectively and in how to provide timely, precise, performance feedback. I find that few organizations provide their managers training in positive leadership. This is unfortunate since positive leadership is a learned skill rather than a natural one. Many texts on performance management are available, such as Aubrey Daniels' *Performance Management: Improving Quality and Productivity Through Positive Reinforcement*; *Goal-Setting: A Motivational Technique*; and Karen Pryor's *Don't Shoot the Dog: The New Art of Teaching and Training* [3].

I once designed a performance feedback system for a restaurant chain. Sales and service goals were established for the "wait teams" that consisted of the food server, cocktail server, and busser. At the end of each shift, the manager was to review each team's results and provide feedback. The managers found this assignment unnatural and bothersome. 6.4 One manager said to me, "I don't like this performance management stuff. It seems artificial. I like to treat my employees as friends."

I pointed out that management was a professional business activity — not a social event. It was his job to provide feedback. After several discussions, he reluctantly agreed. At the end of the next day's shift he met with each team and awarded every member a silver dollar for a job well done.

57

He never looked at the teams' performance records — he simply said "well done" to everyone regardless of their performance!

At another restaurant in the chain, the manager had heard about the introduction of feedback systems and decided to develop his own before I arrived. He created the "keep your job contest" in which the sales of each server were posted each night on a yellow poster board. The rules were that anyone remaining at the bottom of the sales ranking for three consecutive shifts would be fired! This manager could have benefited from positive leadership training.

Management Entropy. The thermodynamic principle of "entropy" states that energy must be applied to a system for the system to be maintained. Systems naturally drift toward chaos without an energy source. If we don't clean our house, mow our yard, service our car, or file our papers, chaos occurs. This principle applies to management as well. If some outside energy is not consistently applied, management practices drift naturally to a "least effort" condition. That least-effort condition is to fail to manage at all, or to ignore employees until something goes wrong.

Positive leadership training alone is not sufficient. The first several years I consulted, I installed performance feedback systems without performance pay. These systems usually produced immediate, and often dramatic, improvements in employee performance across all kinds of jobs and job functions. The problem with these programs was that they were difficult to sustain. Supervisors and managers would enthusiastically manage their performance feedback systems for a month or so and then let them slide. When they did, performance levels would return to their original status. The programs were essentially a "flash in the pan."

When I began to pay incentives for meeting the goals, it quickly became clear that the performance pay payments would sustain my performance feedback programs. Without performance pay, the feedback systems relied totally on the social skills and good will of the supervisor. In a few cases, this was enough and these systems were maintained. But in most, "backup" reinforcers were needed to maintain the system.

6.5 A critical misconception about performance pay should be addressed here. It is not the performance payment that guides or motivates performance improvement — it is the performance feedback associated with the payment. If you had to choose between installing a performance feedback system or a performance pay plan, I would recommend installing the feedback system. Annual bonuses and profit sharing are *not* performance feedback systems. They don't tell employees who, what, when, where, or how. Most performance pay system failures can be attributed to poorly designed feedback systems — not the amount of money paid out.

6.6 Anyone who has tried to collect performance data, for whatever purpose, knows how difficult it is to get consistent and accurate data over time. People forget to collect the data, complain about the effort required to get the data, and fail to turn in the data. Contrast this situation with the sales reports of commissioned salesmen. It is much easier and more natural to get the data when employees are paid on it. Or, contrast the situation with hourly employees who must turn in time sheet hours. These data are generally turned in

59

accurately and on time. Since I began tying performance data to performance pay, I have found that performance feedback systems I install are much more sustainable. I have even had clients tell me that incentives are worth paying just to get timely and accurate performance data! Performance pay is the outside "energy" that prevents management "entropy."

For an employee to consistently perform well, these six questions must be answered:

"Who should do it?"

"What's expected?"

"When is it expected?"

"Where should I do it?"

"How am I doing?"

"Why should I do it?"

Job expectations	Performance feedback	Performance consequence
What's expected?		
Who should do it?	How am I doing?	Why should
When and where		I do it?
should it be done?		

Who, What, When, and Where. Employees are able to accomplish a task only when they understand who is responsible for doing it, what the task is, when it is due, and, in some cases, where it is to be done. In the conventional management system, job requirements are typically specified in formal job descriptions and informally through directives from the supervisor and other employees. The precision of formal job descriptions varies widely across organizations. Many companies simply don't go to the trouble to write job descriptions. Others wrote them years ago, but don't update them, so they have little to do with the current job requirements.

We once designed a performance pay system to improve a bank's customer service in its Automatic Teller Machine (ATM) department. The nine employees we were working with were ATM customer service representatives. Each ATM had a phone that allowed the customer to call these employees when they were having trouble with the machine.

To get some idea of the current service quality, I decided to tape-record a week's worth of conversations for the nine service representatives. The next week we held a meeting with the Vice President of Operations and listened to a sample of the calls. The first call was from a customer who was very agitated. It was raining and the location of the machine was such that the customer was getting wet. "I keep putting my card in the machine and it keeps telling me it's invalid! What should I do?" The answer was, "Wipe it on your butt."

The second call was another eyeopener. "I've got to get to the airport and your machine is out of operation. I must have the cash. What should I do!" Again, without hesitation another representative said, "The branch at Fifth and Oak is close to you and has an ATM." She went on to give detailed directions for the customer to get from his location to Fifth and Oak. This was great, except the branch had closed down over a year ago!

61

We found out quickly that no one had told the customer service representatives the correct answers to most customer questions. The "wipe it on your butt" response was based on a theory among the operators that cards didn't work right because the magnetic stripe had an electrostatic charge. No one had told the representatives about the branch closing. Given no precise job guide, the representatives were simply doing the best they could under the circumstances.

Job expectations should be specified as desired job results rather than simply activities that produce the results. The specification should include what the desired result is, who is supposed to produce the result, by when, and, sometimes, where it is to be produced.

How am I doing? For anyone to learn a job, and then perform the job consistently well, they must be provided performance "feedback." The conventional management system typically provides formal feedback only once a year in the annual performance appraisal. Learning research tells us the ideal delay between a performance and feedback is under three seconds! Once a year certainly doesn't meet this requirement. Not only is typical feedback too delayed, it is usually vague. Most annual appraisals are subjective impressions of the supervisor. Things like "works well with others," "productive," "professional," etc., are rated by the supervisor. Clearly, the formal appraisal system fails as an adequate performance feedback system. Annual appraisals are like trying to play golf in the dark!

However, most organizations augment the annual review with more timely, informal feedback from the supervisor. The frequency and precision of this feedback varies widely with each supervisor. I was meeting with a client's management group to discuss the results of their performance pay system. Several line managers had been invited to the meeting for their reactions. One of them spoke up early in the meeting. "Why do we receive monthly reports on how well each of our employees is meeting her goals? I don't even talk to my employees once a month!" I waited for a response from senior management. Instead, everyone simply nodded in agreement. I wondered what this organization meant when it used the word "management"?

Why should I do it? Even organizations that do maintain formal job descriptions often take the wrong approach. Instead of listing the job *results* the company requires, they only list the job activities. When employees are only told *what* to do, and not *why*, they may develop the wrong job priorities or none at all. Without a knowledge of *why* a task is performed, employees cannot improve the process since the process is all they know.

Try this experiment. Prepare a test over the basic ways your organization makes money. Give the test to your employees and see how many of them pass it. When we have tried this with clients, we find that few people, other than senior management, really understand how the company operates or makes a profit. It is frightening to realize that hundreds or thousands of people are busy doing things without understanding why. John Case, in his *Open-Book Management* [4], extensively describes the benefits of telling employees the "why" of job expectations.

Employee Empowerment. The practice of "management by perception" puts the employee under the personal control of their supervisors. It's not what you accomplish that matters,

63

but whom you impress. If I fail to get a raise or promotion, it's because my supervisor didn't like me or liked someone else better. Unfortunately, these excuses have some validity in the conventional workplace. Subjective annual reviews do make succeeding in the organization a sort of personality contest.

If we really want empowered employees, employees who take responsibility, employees who don't require, or want, constant supervision, then we must replace the conventional subjective annual performance review with objective job result specifications. Sloganeering and cajoling employees to take responsibility hasn't worked and won't work. What's needed is a fundamental change in the management of the workplace. We need to give up the ancient command and control model of management, and engineer a workplace where employees work as entrepreneurs toward objectively defined results. A workplace where employees know how they are performing every day, know why their job results are important to the organization, and share in the organization's success. Such a system will be outlined in the final five chapters.

References

[1] Aubrey C. Daniels and Theodore A. Rosen. *Performance Management: Improving Quality and Productivity Through Positive Reinforcement.* Tucker, GA: Performance Management Publications, 1984.

[2] Edwin A. Locke and Gary P. Latham. *Goal-Setting: A Motivational Technique that Works.* Englewood Cliffs, NJ: Prentice-Hall, 1984.

[3] Karen Pryor. *Don't Shoot the Dog: The New Art of Teaching and Training.* New York: Bantam Books, 1985.

[4] John Case. *Open-Book Management.* New York: Harper-Collins, 1995.

Chapter 7: Management By Exception

MANY MANAGERS BELIEVE THE WAGE AND SALARY SYSTEM IS A RE-
WARD SYSTEM. OTHERS BELIEVE PAY HAS LITTLE OR NO RELATION-
SHIP TO PERFORMANCE AND THAT EMPLOYEES SHOULD BE
"SELF-MOTIVATED." IN FACT, CONVENTIONAL PAY MAINTAINS EM-
PLOYEE PERFORMANCE THROUGH INTIMIDATION. EMPLOYEES DON'T
WORK TO RECEIVE THEIR PAYCHECKS, THEY WORK TO *AVOID LOSING
THEM*!

Pay and Performance. Many people argue that wages and
salaries are, in themselves, an incentive to work. However,
an incentive arrangement states, "If you do A, you will get
B." Conventional pay doesn't work this way. It says, "Each
payday you'll get B until you don't do A."

Incentive   If A, then B

Wage/Salary   B until no A

         (A is result and B is pay)

In conventional pay systems people work not to earn their
pay, but to avoid losing it (getting demoted or fired). This
approach to management is termed "management by exception." To determine if your company's pay system is actually
tied to performance, apply the "dead man rule." If one of
your salaried employees dropped dead, but no one informed
your payroll department, would the dead employee be mailed
a check on payday? If yes, then your pay system is obviously
not tied to performance!

66

Lazy Management. Management through intimidation is a natural way to manage the behavior of others. "If you don't clean up your room, no car tonight!" "If you don't pay attention you will have to stay after school!" If you don't pay your taxes you will go to jail!" "If you don't perform, we will fire you!" The reason this approach to managing others is natural is that it's easy and it reduces an unpleasant emotional state — anger. It's easy because managers don't have to go to the trouble to specify what job outcomes they want. Further, they don't have to track employee performance or provide continuous feedback. Management by exception allows managers and supervisors to basically ignore their subordinates until they fail to perform.

One comment I hear from managers when I describe performance management is, "I'll be so busy specifying job outcomes and providing employees with performance feedback, I won't have time to manage!" It's always unclear to me what is meant by management in this statement.

Unfortunately, management by exception substantially reduces employee performance. Research finds a median 30 percent improvement in employee performance, and often as high as 300 percent, with the introduction of precise job expectations and performance feedback. Management by exception is lazy management. It is a technique that allows managers to avoid the difficult part of management: defining who is responsible for what, when, and where; informing employees how they are doing; and communicating why they are asked to do it. The lost employee potential caused by management by exception can only be imagined.

Management by exception also "feels" good. We manage mistakes, or failures to produce, when we are angry. The anger automatically energizes us to act. The "management" reduces our anger. Specifying desired outcomes and providing feedback is a logical, rather than an emotional, process. It is not as emotionally satisfying to the supervisor to manage performance as it is to manage exceptions.

Self-Motivation. In his book, *Punished by Rewards* [1], Alfie Kohn argues that paying employees incentives is manipulative and damages the employee's natural sense of accomplishment. The late Edward Deming, the quality expert, also argued against performance pay in *Out of the Crisis* [2]. Reading these criticisms is, to me, akin to reading the pronouncements of the "Flat Earth Society."

These authors' arguments are logical within their own construction, but start from a flawed premise. This premise is that people are "self-motivated." This view of employee motivation still dominates our schools of management and is loosely based on "self-actualization" and the "hierarchy of needs" as proposed by the clinical psychologist Abraham Maslow in his book *Motivation and Personality* [3].

The idea that we are self-motivated is a cherished idea, at least in our Western culture. A full discussion of this issue can be found in Skinner's *Beyond Freedom and Dignity* [4]. For our purposes here, suffice it to say that self-motivation, as a management principle for business organizations, is both useless and illogical. It is useless in that it explains everything and nothing. It is circular reasoning to say an employee did or didn't perform because he did or didn't want to. How do we know he wanted to? Because he did it. Why did he do it? Because he wanted to.

The concept of self-motivation has encouraged management to think about motivation in the wrong way and to implement performance improvement strategies that have never worked, and won't work. If people are self-motivated, then the management of employee performance comes down to nothing more than hiring the right people.

"Wanted: self-starters" is a common employment ad. If they existed, would we really even want self-motivated employees? Motivated to do what? If they are truly self-motivated, then the objectives of the organization are irrelevant unless they just happen to be in line with the employee's "self-objectives." The idea of hundreds of self-motivated, self-directed employees is frightening. It sounds like a mob rather than an organization.

We like to think we are personally self-motivated. We don't like the idea that others influence our behavior. But if people are not influenced by others, how can an organization operate toward common objectives? How can people cooperatively work toward a common goal when all goals are personal? What is the purpose of managers and supervisors? The self-motivation promoters answer that we must *persuade* employees that the organization's goals should be their own. We'll put slogans on the wall. We'll sing company songs together. We'll hold team meetings. We'll get in touch with our feelings in sensitivity training. We'll bring in motivational speakers. We'll go on retreats together. We'll climb mountains together. If these things don't work, and they won't — we'll fire them!

Management theorists typically devote little text to describing the conventional pay system and its relationship to employee performance. The view is that people work and, oh, by the way, they get paid. Some of this thinking stems from the well-known work of Elton Mayo and others at the Hawthorne Electric plant in the 1940s. They concluded that employee performance was not related to pay, but rather to the company's social environment. A second source for this view is job satisfaction surveys in which respondents ranked pay as a low concern and supervisory practices as the highest concern.

It is really no surprise that employees are more interested in the way they are supervised than in their pay. Most of us concern ourselves with things we can do something about. Conventional pay is a monolith. The employee can do little to increase his pay. The only route available for additional pay and promotions is through the supervisor (management by perception).

More importantly, the only way pay is reduced, or eliminated, is also through the supervisor (management by exception). The original job satisfaction surveys in which pay was a low concern were administered to employees who were primarily paid wages. *INC* magazine sent similar surveys to self-employed and commissioned salespeople and found the primary concern to be personal earnings, not supervision.

If pay is really of little interest to your employees, try this experiment. Announce on Friday there will be no paychecks beginning next week and see who shows up for work on Monday. If they are truly self-motivated, they'll still show up. I have puzzled over why so many management theorists insist there is no link between pay and employee performance, or want to make employee motivation a mysterious inner force, when the natural link between pay and performance seems so obvious. This advocacy parallels Marxian theory that wishes to decouple individuals from the fruits of their labor and gives "to each according to their needs, and from each according to their abilities."

The view that people require an intermediary between their efforts and the resulting rewards is an elitist position. It is an elitist idea that people must have a politician or bureaucrat intercede between people and their earnings through taxation and redistribution. It is also an elitist idea that workers must have supervisors intercede to determine how much pay they will receive for their efforts. It is a self-serving idea, since without it we would have no need for intercessionaries like politicians, bureaucrats, lawyers, counselors, social workers and, in business organizations, supervisors. The philosopher, Ayn Rand, has written extensively on this topic in novels such as *Atlas Shrugged* [5].

Coercion. People do not require "extrinsic" motivation to engage in tasks that are inherently entertaining (playing the piano) or satisfying (eating a good meal). All of us know this. That is why we call these tasks hobbies or play. Other tasks we perform are not inherently entertaining or satisfying. We perform these tasks to earn something we do value such as money, or to prevent aversive events (such as changing the oil in our car). We call these tasks work. Most of us make this distinction between work and play easily. Some management theorists, however, have argued that all tasks should be play (intrinsically motivating) and none work. This position is found in "job enrichment" programs and the like. It's a nice

71

idea, but how many of us would file documents or load trucks for the fun of it!

B. F. Skinner defined the two reasons we work as "positive reinforcement" and "negative reinforcement" [6]. Most of us intuitively understand positive reinforcement, though we are sometimes confused about its most efficient application. On the other hand, negative reinforcement is widely misunderstood and misstated. Negative reinforcement is often confused with punishment in many management and psychology texts. Negative reinforcement has the opposite effect of punishment on performance. The operational definitions of behavioral consequences that determine whether a performance will be repeated are:

Positive reinforcement: Increasing and maintaining the frequency of performance through the application of desirable factors.

Negative reinforcement: Increasing and maintaining the frequency of performance through the removal of aversive factors.

Positive Punishment: Reducing the frequency of behaviors through the application of aversive factors.

Negative Punishment: Reducing the frequency of behaviors through the removal of desirable factors.

Though these definitions are straightforward, the practical application of these principles is complicated by the personal histories (and possibly genetic makeup) of each employee. What is desirable and what is aversive will differ somewhat from person to person. A person whose parents' attention was always followed by punishment may find supervisor attention threatening and undesirable. A person whose parents' attention usually meant something good would follow will likely find supervisor attention desirable.

These personal differences occur most often with interpersonal factors such as recognition, since these vary the most widely in people's experiences. Money, however, is less likely to vary in its direct effects on people and is a "generalized" reinforcer since it can be exchanged for most anything of value to the individual, regardless of her unique personal history.

Management by exception relies on negative reinforcement to get people to perform. Negative reinforcement does work. It is easier to use, natural, reinforcing to the supervisor, and it often improves performance more quickly than positive reinforcement. Slave labor relied on negative reinforcement. If you failed to work, you were whipped. You worked to avoid these things from happening to you.

Management in wage and salary systems sometimes involves punishment through the application of aversive factors such as supervisor reprimands, poor performance reviews or assignments to undesirable tasks. More often, though, management uses negative reinforcement to get people to work through the threat of removing something of value to the employee if he fails to perform. These threats include demotions and loss of status, no pay increase, no promotion, suspensions without pay, cutbacks in hours, reassignment from favored shifts, assignment to low-opportunity sales territories, and ultimately, termination. These are the real management tools in a wage and salary system!

You may be thinking, "But very little of this sort of thing goes on in my company. I can't remember the last time someone was fired. This can't be the way we manage employees." And you would be accurate. In most companies, the actual application of aversive factors is rare. But, these are still the controlling variables. Employees are simply successful in avoiding the aversive factors by performing sufficiently to prevent their application. It is because negative reinforcement works through avoidance that it is so difficult to observe or to understand its operation.

Drive down any highway and you will observe that most people are driving at the approximate speed limit. Is this because they enjoy driving at the speed limit? No, it is to avoid a traffic ticket. Even though we may only occasionally see someone getting a traffic ticket, our driving is "managed" by the *threat* of a ticket all the same. This is how negative reinforcement most commonly operates to manage behavior.

A quality expert from Japan related the story of an emperor of Japan who created the "99 rules of good conduct." His samurai warriors enforced the code. If a citizen violated one of the 99 rules he was removed from his home by the samurai, taken to the center of the town square, and his head was chopped off. But what made the rules especially effective was that they were never published! No one was sure what all the rules were, or when they might be in violation of them.

Consequently, everyone played things pretty close to the vest. As you can imagine, there was little display of personal initiative or creativity in this society. How many of our organizations have their own "99 rules"? How many of our organizations stifle individual initiative and creativity with their 99 rules?

The following is a personal experience with negative reinforcement. Some years ago I was asked to teach a performance management course to prison guards. I was having some difficulty in explaining the concepts of positive and negative reinforcement so I decided to conduct a demonstration. I brought two white rats and two "Operant Chambers."

An Operant Chamber is a Plexiglas box about one foot wide, long and high. Inside the box is a small bar that moves up and down. The training objective is to teach the rat to press the bar with its paw. To one box I added a food dispenser that would deliver a pellet of food by a switch I controlled, or the rat could deliver the food by pressing the bar. In the second box, rather than a food dispenser, the floor of the box was a grid of steel bars that was attached to a shock generator. I could turn off the shock from a switch I had, or the rat could prevent the shock onset by pressing the bar.

The box with the food dispenser was designed to demonstrate positive reinforcement. The box with the shock grid was designed to demonstrate negative reinforcement. I began my demonstration with positive reinforcement. Each time the rat approached the bar I triggered the delivery of a food pellet. Then I waited until he came closer to the bar, then touched the bar, and so on, until the rat pressed the bar and fed himself (a training technique termed "shaping"). It took about thirty minutes to train the rat to press the bar for food.

I then moved to the negative reinforcement demonstration. When the shock came on, the second rat, by accident, jumped directly onto the bar and turned the shock off. After the onset of only a few additional shocks, the rat was pressing the bar to prevent future shocks. It took about five minutes to train the rat to press the bar to prevent a shock. When I asked the guards about the effectiveness of these two procedures, they pointed out that the negative reinforcement worked much quicker and didn't cost me any food. Needless to say, I was disappointed in the results of my demonstration. Rather than train the guards in positive ways to manage prisoner behavior, I had simply reinforced their original view of management through intimidation.

During the break, one of the guards opened the positively reinforced rat's box, removed the rat, and begin petting it. Another guard saw this and decided to play with the negatively reinforced rat. This was a serious mistake. When he put his hand in the box, the rat immediately bit into his finger. He began slinging the rat around wildly but could not get loose. Finally, we extracted the rat from his finger and things quieted down. I then asked the guards what they had learned. One guard spoke up and said, "You can get someone to do what you want through negative reinforcement — you just don't want to be around them much!"

I don't want to stretch the rat analogy too far, but imagine you are running these experiments over several weeks. Each morning you go to the rats' "home" cages to get them for today's training session. When you reach in to pick up the positively reinforced rat do you think it is eager or reluctant to come to you? It is eager to "go to work" and actually jumps into your hands since it will be fed in the training session. On the other hand, is the negatively reinforced rat equally as eager to "go to work"? No; in fact you have to wear special gloves to avoid getting bitten. Further, you have to pry the rat's claws from the bottom of the cage to get them free from the cage. Though we understand people aren't rats, do you find your employees are more like the positively or negatively reinforced rats?

If you had both rats in their Operant Chambers, you would see two rats pressing bars with their paws. If you invited someone to observe, who had not been in the original training sessions, he would see no difference in the two rats' behaviors or situations. This is why so many people find it difficult to understand what motivates employee performance and how the organization relates to it.

Not only is negative reinforcement more natural and less effort, it can continue to control a person's behavior long after its actual application has ceased. This phenomenon is termed "avoidance behavior." We are bitten by a dog and avoid all dogs thereafter. Since we avoid dogs we are never bitten again but also fail to learn that not all dogs bite. It's like the old joke about the guy who performs some ritual to keep the elephants away. When told there aren't any elephants in town he says "See, it works!" Avoidance behavior is at the root of many neuroses like obsessive hand-washing and phobias such as claustrophobia. A single powerful event can maintain an irrational fear the rest of a person's life.

We learn to act appropriately as children to avoid our parents' displeasure or punishment. We learn to study to avoid bad grades. We learn to conform as teenagers to avoid ridicule. We learn to obey the law to avoid fines or jail.

Though positive reinforcement is also used at home, in school, and in society, it is more often the exception than the rule. Negative reinforcement or aversive control is unfortunately the more natural way we use to control others. We tend to ignore people until they fail to do what we want.

Since this failure often causes us to be angry, our natural response is to strike out. As long as things go our way we don't act. This is why positive reinforcement is so seldom used.

Service Quality and Negative Reinforcement. Each year, and especially in recent years, companies spend millions of dollars on quality improvement programs. Many of these programs emphasize training managers and workers in team processes aimed at developing better methods and procedures that will lead to service and quality improvements. The results of quality circles and the like have been mixed. I think the reason these results have not been consistently positive is largely attributable to a basic oversight in the approach — *many employees have no reason to give good service!*

Why is service so slow? We have designed performance pay plans for several banks. The bank teller is one of the key contact points customers have with their bank. Many customers' chief impressions of their bank come from the quality of service they receive from the teller. As the reader likely knows from personal experience, teller service is often slow and impersonal. Why? Do tellers not know how to smile at customers and provide eager and efficient service? Many bankers think so and spend substantial dollars training tellers how to be courteous.

But let's step back from the situation a minute. People tend to do what's in their best interests. Tellers receive modest hourly wages and some sort of annual increase, regardless of how many customers they serve. Rather than being measured on how many customers they serve, tellers are measured on their "shortages." Their cash drawers must balance at the end of the day. If they fail to balance too often, they are fired.

78

What is the best way to avoid having shortages and getting fired? Don't wait on any customers! You can't have a shortage, or make a mistake, if you don't serve any customers. Given the way the bank measures teller performance and pays tellers, it's no surprise customers often experience slow service. In fact, I've told bankers that if they see a teller waiting on a lot of customers, they should at least have the decency to pull her aside and explain the rules of the game to her.

One of our mottoes is "Dead men make no errors." If you never do anything, you can never foul up. Since many organizations find out about errors, but fail to measure the volume of work performed, it is no surprise their employees are reluctant to wait on customers. Try this test. Go into any retail establishment. If the salespeople run at you, you'll find they are on commission. If they run from you, you'll find they are on wages or a salary.

Until the company ties employee pay to serving customers, no amount of training or "sloganeering" will permanently improve customer service. Management must align employees' personal motives with the organization's. In my consulting with the restaurant chain, it came up during a meeting that one of the managers was disturbed at the number of reports of poor quality from his region's restaurants. Angrily he asked, "How is it we provide the best training and resources in the industry and yet we are consistently outperformed by competing Mom and Pop restaurants?" We all thought about this for awhile and finally one manager said, "Maybe it's because our managers are salaried, but each lost customer comes right out of Mom's and Pop's wallets!" Salaries and prompt service don't mix well.

Why is service so uncreative? Have you ever been told, "It's not company policy; I can't do anything about it; I'll have to call my manager; it's not my department; or it's not my job." Why is this? Most companies pay fairly. Why won't employees treat their customers well? Don't they see that their jobs depend upon the company being profitable? The answer is that wages and salaries are a fear-based management system that causes employees to be anxious and to avoid decision-making. Rather than seeing each customer as an opportunity, the employee sees each customer as a liability — nothing more than a chance to make an error and suffer the consequences.

Managing Through Fear. Many managers believe salary to be a positive reinforcer. "They ought to work; they're paid to," is a frequent comment. But are employees really paid to work? Positive reinforcement means pay must be "contingent" on performance. That is, when you perform well, you are compensated, but when you don't perform well, you are not.

Factory piecework and sales commissions (ignoring other problems) are good examples of pay applied as positive reinforcement. The more you produce, the more you are paid. Salaries and wages, in contrast, only remotely relate to day-to-day performance. The salary remains the same both in the amount and frequency of payment as long as the employee performs above minimum standards.

Wages and salaries do generally ensure minimum levels of performance. But this is only true when an immediate supervisor enforces the minimum standard. Without supervisors, employees could conceivably perform no work at all and still receive their pay. It is the supervisor who translates salaries into performance contingencies. The two components work hand-in-hand. Without a wage or salary, the supervisor would have little control over employees. Without the supervisor, the wage exerts little control over performance.

In most organizations, the supervisor can readily reduce or remove an employee's pay through suspensions, demotions, cutbacks in hours, poor performance reviews and ultimately termination. The supervisor can only increase an employee's pay once a year through a "merit increase" or promotion. This increase is typically tightly controlled and limited.

Further, the entitlement culture has fostered an employee group that views annual pay increases as an entitlement. Rather than perceiving an increase as a reward, the employee more often sees the supervisor as able to reduce the increase for poor performance. In fact, even annual pay increases operate more often as threats that they will not be awarded, than rewards for exceptional performance.

How to use pay to scare the hell out of employees! In the conventional organization the supervisor must rely on negative reinforcement (intimidation) to motivate employees. Since this is the case, the following advice is offered to optimize the supervisor's ability to motivate employees (tongue-in-cheek, of course).

Management Through Fear: Pay Guidelines.

1. Pay more than other companies. All people spend up to, or above, their incomes. The fear of losing this standard of living produces peak performance and inextricably binds the employee to the organization.

81

2. Hire people with lots of dependents. They have more to lose if you fire them.

3. Hire less job-mobile employees who have few alternatives to working for you.

4. Introduce "benefits" such as health insurance and retirement plans. These encourage employees to not prepare for emergencies and to become totally dependent on the good graces of your supervisors.

5. Provide "status" titles and perks when money is in short supply. To some people, loss of status is as frightening as the loss of cold cash.

6. Base salary increases on tenure rather than performance. Most people realize it's a sure bet they'll get older. By making a job secure, the employee becomes less able to deal with uncertainty and the threat of termination is enhanced.

After the above guidelines have been met, the final step is to train your supervisors in how to be optimally intimidating. Unpredictability is a key ingredient in the ability to intimidate. Once this skill has been mastered, the supervisor will be able to maintain consistent above-standard performance through high levels of employee anxiety.

The leadership quality of unpredictability is highly prized in organizations that manage through fear. Nothing enhances the maintenance of fear as much as putting quick-tempered, arbitrary people in control of an employee's livelihood. For fledgling supervisors, some suggestions to improve unpredictability are provided.

7.9

Management Through Fear: Supervision Guidelines.

1. Interact with your employees based on your mood — but not always.

2. Occasionally praise or promote an obviously inferior performer to assert your absolute control of the situation.

3. Conversely, publicly criticize your best performer for some minor infraction. This really confuses the group.

4. Fire someone. Some random approach such as the "termination dart board" is best. Terminations, to effectively produce fear in the remaining employees, must be illogical and unanticipated.

5. Offer no direction to your employee group. Or, offer specific direction and change your mind once a week. Then criticize your subordinates for not getting the job done.

6. Establish performance goals and then write performance reviews on totally unrelated criteria. Employees must be taught that your personal whim controls their destinies.

7. Never praise good employees. Employees will begin to feel competent and comfortable in their jobs. As anxiety drops, so will your control of their performance.

8. To keep employees from getting the impression they are doing satisfactory work, performance standards should be nonexistent or at least highly ambiguous. In this way, no matter how well an employee performs, he is kept completely in the dark and therefore anxious and productive.

9. Comment on performance errors only. Ignore competent performers and focus on criticizing poor performers. An ideal opportunity to reinforce your authority is to raise hell

over an error committed by a conscientious worker. This sets an example for others that you can never be satisfied, thus maintaining your power to intimidate.

References

[1] Alfie Kohn. *Punished by Rewards.* New York: Houghton Mifflin, 1993.

[2] W. Edwards Deming. *Out of the Crisis.* Cambridge, MA: MIT, 1982.

[3] A.H. Maslow. *Motivation and Personality.* New York: Harper, 1954.

[4] B.F. Skinner. *Beyond Freedom and Dignity.* New York: Alfred A. Knopf, 1971.

[5] Ayn Rand. *Atlas Shrugged.* New York: Random House, 1957.

[6] B. F. Skinner. *The Behavior of Organisms.* New York: Appleton-Century, 1938.

Chapter 8: Entitlement Thinking

ENTITLEMENT THINKING IS A NATIONAL PROBLEM AND IS PERVASIVE IN OUR WORKPLACES. IT IS A SOCIALISTIC VIEW THAT FOSTERS MINIMUM PERFORMANCE AND AN UNWILLINGNESS TO ACCEPT PERSONAL ACCOUNTABILITY.

There is much discussion today about empowered employees, self-directed work teams, and flat organizations. The definition of empowerment seems to be giving employees the ability to make decisions without their having to accept the consequences or to benefit from them. We want choices without accountability. This problem appears to be a culture-wide issue rather than just a workplace issue. Several authors have written about our unwillingness to accept accountability. These sources include: *Culture of Complaint: The Fraying of America,* Robert Hughes [1], *Working Without a Net*, Morris R. Shechtman [2], *A Nation of Victims: The Decay of the American Character*, Charles J. Sykes [3], *Blue Monday*, Robert Eisenberger [4], and the granddaddy of them all, William H. Whyte's *The Organization Man* [5].

The common theme of these authors is that people refuse to accept accountability for their actions. "It's not my fault" is the signature comment. The roots of this development are thought to be in the disintegration of the family, the school system, the decline of religion, and "big brother" government. I would add another that is rarely mentioned — the entitlement workplace.

Entitlement pay refers to the view held by many employees, and even employers, that for simply showing up and meeting minimum job requirements, an employee deserves his pay. This view is widespread. It's interesting to think about the term now in vogue for pay — compensation. In the courts we are compensated for damages and pain inflicted upon us by others. It is revealing that this term now applies to pay in the workplace.

A common misinterpretation of our Bill of Rights is that we have a right to security and a good living. The right is to the *opportunity* to secure these things, not the things themselves. Recent legislation to prevent companies from discriminatory hiring on bases other than performance are in line with our founding fathers' philosophy. However, it is fallacious to expand the definition of discrimination to include poor performance. No one has a right to share in the profits of an organization when he fails to contribute to its success.

Entitlement thinking and "victim" thinking permeate today's society. If I fail to perform, it is not my fault; it is always someone else's fault. This is a radical change in our country's work ethic and our general view of personal accountability. How did it occur? In the workplace I believe it is a natural outgrowth of the conventional pay system, which treats people as interchangeable commodities.

The phenomenon of "learned helplessness" was studied over many years by the psychologist Martin Seligman [6]. In his early animal research he would train a laboratory rat to press a lever to receive food. After the rat had learned to press the bar to receive food, a bowl of food was placed in the cage. When the rat had experienced free access to the bowl of food, the bowl was removed. Surprisingly the rat went hungry rather than returning to pressing the lever for food. The connection between the rat's "job" and the food had been lost. In another set of experiments, the rat pressed the lever to turn off a shock grid in the cage. A lamp was illuminated just before the shock was applied. If the rat pressed the lever, the shock was avoided. The rat quickly learned to press the lever when the lamp was lit and successfully avoided the shock. In the second phase of the experiment, the shock was applied even when the rat pressed the lever. After several trials in which the rat could not avoid the shock, the original contingencies were reinstituted. The rat never learned the "rules" had reverted and passively received the shock rather than press the bar to avoid it. The rat learned to be helpless.

Today, a majority of employees are paid fixed wages and salaries. Often, a government-dictated or company-sponsored benefits program accompanies the wage or salary. Each year employee performance is reviewed and an annual increase to the base pay is applied. In some organizations this basic pay package is augmented by annual profit sharing or bonus plans. The employer often assists the employee in saving through a pension plan, provides health insurance, and pays the employees' taxes through withholding. These entitlements and government-directed paternalism create an employee group too dependent upon the company — a learned helplessness.

Although you can trace the concept of salary to the Roman army, and the advent of modern wages to Henry Ford, our present wage and salary system fully came into its own after World War II. Today's wage and salary system developed in an era when there was a severe shortage of labor, and we were the only sellers while the rest of the world were buyers. Fifty years later, our businesses are shackled with this outmoded pay system that severely restricts our ability to compete in today's world markets. It is a pay system that encourages employee "entitlement" thinking, discourages employee initiative and creativity, and defeats any sense of personal accomplishment.

In his book *The Spirit of Enterprise* [7], George Gilder describes the different perspectives of entrepreneurs and entitlement thinkers toward work.

> *But like the barbarians of Ortega's vision in Revolt of the Masses, many children of the West assume that they are entitled: that the comforts of life are natural and inevitable while its hardships are an effect of the malignity of dialectics or exogenous sciences rather than contrived by the specific exertions and sacrifices of men and women on the frontiers of enterprise.*
>
> *While the entitled children ache at the burden of laboring nine to five, the entrepreneurs rise before dawn and work happily from five to nine. While the entitled children complain that success comes from 'contacts' with the high and mighty — and talk of the frustrations of 'politics' — the entrepreneurs ignore politics and make their contacts with workers and customers. While the entitled children see failure as catastrophe — a reason to resign — the entrepreneur takes it in stride as a spur to new struggle.*

Just as our country's wealth and social policies have fostered an entitlement culture, so has the conventional wage and salary system fostered an entitlement culture in our businesses.

88

It has created a corporate socialism that rewards mediocrity while punishing individual initiative and creativity. Over the past twenty years, I have spent my time working with companies to change this system. The more time I spend examining our current wage and salary system, the more pervasive I find its detrimental effects on businesses and other types of organizations with payrolls.

For several years I have conducted public seminars across the country on performance pay. These seminars are attended chiefly by owners and senior managers of business organizations. Although over one thousand people have attended the seminar, I have yet to find *one* defender of the way we pay people. We all know it's wrong, and it's time to do something about it — and do it now.

If so few support the present entitlement pay system, then why is it still so pervasive? Partly because of simple inertia — we know how to do it. Partly because of a failure of managers to understand the seriousness of the problems the system causes. Partly because it's relatively easy to administer. Partly because, despite our lip-service to employee empowerment, the current system is an autocratic system that keeps our employees passive and pliable.

We exchange ease of management for poor performance. The conventional pay system is paternalistic. The employee is guaranteed a base pay, vacations, and personal days. His insurance and retirement are often handled by the company. Many companies have all sorts of required social events, creating one big happy family. Do any of us really want this much "company"?

The employee pays dearly for this cradle-to-grave parenting. Just as a child living at home, he gives up his personal autonomy. He is dependent upon the company. It is a system not too different from the coal mine's "company store" where workers became so indebted to the company, to quit was to risk going to jail. Ernie Banks, a major league baseball coach, summed up this approach to management by saying, "I like players to be married and in debt. That's the way you motivate them."

Since World War II, many companies have evolved into socialistic organizations whose employees have come to view pay and benefits as entitlements. As evidenced by events in Eastern Europe, and across the globe, socialism doesn't work. It has proven grossly inefficient in the production and distribution of goods. It is a system that distributes equal pieces of an ever-shrinking pie. It is an inequitable system that fails to reward achievers and sustains shirkers. These flaws were pointed out as early as 1959 by none other than Nikita Khrushchev, the premier of the Soviet Union: "Call it what you will, incentives are what get people to work harder."

We must move away from entitlement thinking and toward a free enterprise or capitalist view of management *inside* our organizations. Too many entrepreneurs build companies so autocratic and paternalistic that they would never work in them. The American worker is losing (or has lost) the free enterprise philosophy that was the engine of our success. This erosion of our core values began many years ago. William H. Whyte wrote in his 1956 book *The Organization Man*, "Today's challenge, today's dire necessity is to sell — to resell if you will — to free Americans the philosophy that has kept us and our economy free." The flaws in entitlement pay were recognized long before the 1950s. Listen to the Pilgrims as John Smith wrote in 1624:

When our people were fed out of the common store, and labored jointly together, glad was he who could slip from his labor, or slumber over his task he cared not how, nay, the most honest among them would hardly take so much true pains in a week, as now for themselves they will do in a day.

Or John Stuart Mill, *"As a general rule, remuneration by fixed salaries does not in any class of functionaries produce the maximum of zeal."*

And, of course, Adam Smith, the father of capitalism who wrote in 1776:

It is not from the benevolence of the butcher, the brewer, or the baker that we expect our dinner, but from their regard to their interest. We address ourselves, not to their humanity, but to their self-love, and never talk to them of our necessities but of their advantages.

However, forty years of entitlement thinking can't be changed overnight. Years of paternalism have made our employees timid and self-satisfied. Speaking of the country, George Lois says, "Officially we revere free enterprise, initiative and individuality. Unofficially we fear it." How do we get employees to take a personal stake in their jobs and the success of the company? Two common approaches have been profit sharing or employee ownership. Do these strategies really create a true entrepreneurial workplace?

Employee Stock Ownership and Profit Sharing Plans. If we want to move our employee group away from entitlement thinking and toward an entrepreneurial organizational culture, employee stock ownership seems a logical direction to pursue. Unfortunately, the results of employee ownership plans have been sketchy. In the Brookings Institute's *Paying for Productivity: A Look at the Evidence* [8], the editor, Alan S. Binder, states;

What then, do we learn from this important collection of papers? First, there is good reason to believe profit sharing does indeed raise productivity, but much less reason to believe ESOPs do so.... Nonetheless, in true Murphy's Law fashion, the U.S. Government subsidizes ESOPs, but not profit sharing, with tax breaks.

On the other hand, many studies have found weak to moderate relationships between profit sharing plans and improved corporate performance. These studies are well-reviewed and referenced in the Brookings Institute book. Unfortunately, all the studies appear to contain problems in their methods and findings. More research is required to nail down what are the salient characteristics of good profit sharing plans and in what situations profit sharing works best.

* The reader who wants more information on ESOPs and productivity is referred to the US. General Accounting Office, "Employee Stock Ownership Plans: Little Evidence of Effects on Corporate Performance," GAO/ PEMD - 88 -1 (October, 1987), and to Joseph R. Blasi, *Employee Ownership: Revolution or Ripoff?* (Balinger Books, 1988).

References

(1) Robert Hughes. *Culture of Complaint: The Fraying of America.* New York: Oxford University Press, 1993.

(2) Morris R. Shechtman. *Working Without A Net.* Englewood Cliffs, NJ: Prentice Hall, 1994.

(3) Charles J. Sykes. *A Nation of Victims: The Decay of the American Character.* New York: St. Martin's Press, 1992.

(4) Robert Eisenberger. *Blue Monday: The Loss of the Work Ethic in America.* New York: Paragon House, 1989.

(5) William H. Whyte. *The Organization Man.* Garden City, NY: Doubleday and Company, 1957.

(6) M.E.P. Seligman. *Helplessness.* San Francisco: W.H. Freeman, 1975.

(7) George Gilder. *The Spirit of Enterprise.* New York: Simon and Schuster, 1984.

(8) Alan S. Binder (Ed.). *Paying for Productivity: A Look at the Evidence.* Washington, DC: The Brookings Institution, 1990.

Section II:
The Total Performance System

Chapter 9: Problems with Conventional Alternative Pay Plans

9.1 CONVENTIONAL, ALTERNATIVE PAY PLANS FALL INTO TWO CATEGORIES; GROUP PLANS AND PIECEMEAL PLANS THAT ARE GOAL-DRIVEN, PIECE-RATE, OR SALES COMMISSIONS. THESE PLANS FAIL TO ACHIEVE MANY ORGANIZATIONAL OBJECTIVES.

A survey by the Hay Group (*The Hay Report: Compensation and Benefits Strategies for 1995 and Beyond*) [1] found that of those companies surveyed, 41 percent reported increasing their use of performance pay in the last two years. Further, 48 percent used incentives for lower management levels, 39 percent for technical and professional staff, and 27 percent for nonexempt, hourly staff.

9.2 **Objectives of a performance pay system.** An effective performance pay system should provide these benefits to the organization and its employees:

Variable Pay. Shift a portion of pay from a fixed expense to a variable expense indexed to organizational profits. This indexing stabilizes profit margins, increases employee pay opportunity during business upturns, and reduces the risk of layoffs during business downturns.

Improve and Maintain Performance. Provide employees targeted, objective performance goals, timely feedback, and performance-based pay.

Align Employee Goals with the Organization's. Employee objectives, feedback and performance pay should be directly aligned with organizational profitability and strategic objectives.

95

Pay Employees Relative to Contribution. Create a pay system where those who contribute more, earn more.

Create an Entrepreneurial Workplace. Create a pay system that fosters self-managed employees, rewards innovation, and ensures a customer focus.

9.3

Group Performance Pay Plans. A common incentive scheme is the profit-sharing program. Typically, this type of plan pays out annually from a profit pool. The pool is allocated to employees based on their salaries as a percentage of total salaries. (Profit sharing used for retirement plans is not considered in this discussion since its purposes are different.) The Brookings Institution review of annual, profit sharing [2] found little difference in the success of companies that had profit sharing plans vs. those that didn't.

Gainshare plans are often implemented at a sub-level (division or department) of the organization and are therefore "closer" to the participants. Often, gainshare plan payouts are based upon improvements in a cost/unit in which the elements are more under the control of participants than is company profit. For these reasons, the above research did find a modest relationship between company performance and the presence of a gainshare plan. In either case, a group plan will likely have a greater effect on performance if the group is smaller and the elements of the payout formula are more under employee control.

7.4

Group incentive plans typically fail to:

1) specify the results each employee must achieve to make the company successful (fail to align employee and organizational goals).

96

2) provide employees precise, timely performance feedback that is critical to improving and maintaining performance.

3) equitably recognize each employee's personal contribution.

4) create a true worker-manager partnership in which employees share rewards *and risks* through replacing a portion of guaranteed pay with pay indexed to the profitability of the organization.

Piecemeal Incentive Plans. Piecemeal plans include any incentive plans that pay on individual production, such as sales commissions and piece-rate plans. Piecemeal plans are not tied to company results, but rather to the individual employee's results. Piecemeal plans are arguably the most motivating plans since they provide specific performance goals and feedback and they pay employees directly proportionate to their personal contribution. There are two primary problems with these plans.

First, they must exclude all employees who are in job positions that have no identifiable "piece" to pay upon. The consequence is that it is common for the salespeople to earn commissions for sales while those who support them are salaried.

Second, these plans often fail to align the employee's personal objectives with the organization's. My first incentive plan was a piece-rate type of plan for a data entry group. The baseline items-per-hour rate for the group was about 950 net items (net of errors). The initial plan provided daily feedback to each operator, and supervisor recognition, for improvement — but no performance pay. In a few weeks, the rates rose to 1,650 items per hour. Management was so impressed the supervisor was promoted. The new supervisor

97

felt it was too much effort to provide the operators daily feedback and discontinued the program. The rates fell back to around 1,100 items per hour.

We then introduced monetary incentives as an add-on to the base wage. Over a period of a few months, the rates rose to 2,400 items per hour. Later, we moved the system to a true piece-rate in which the base wage was removed and the operators were paid so much per item, minus errors. The result was a 3,100 item-per-hour rate that was maintained over a fifteen-year period.

As an aside, turnover in the initial wage system was 150 percent (everyone left each year and half of the new employees left as well). During the piece-rate system, turnover fell to zero. This was because each operator was earning an average 50 percent more than in the wage system. Further, the group became self-managed, which enabled operators to make a good living within flexible work hours while the company benefited from a lower labor cost per unit.

About six months into the piece-rate system, the company president visited the department to see how the employees liked piece-rate. He sat with one of the operators and asked her if she found the system too stressful or unpredictable and whether she would prefer to return to a conventional wage. The operator stopped processing, looked directly at the president, and said, "You've cost me about six dollars talking to me — how much more do you have to say!"

Further investigation found that the operators were competing with each other and were unwilling to assist new operators. The only activity they would engage in was processing.

If they were asked to help on other tasks, or in other areas, the answer was a resounding "no"!

A similar problem occurs with commissioned salespeople. The stories are legendary of salespeople who discount to the point of no profits; sell things to people who can't pay; and make promises the operations department can't keep! In sum, though piece-rate plans are highly motivational, they appear to have limited applications where individuals work alone and cannot make decisions that are adverse to the company.

The following table compares the various conventional pay plans, and the Total Performance System to be described in the remaining chapters, to the five performance pay objectives.

	Variable Payroll	Perf. Imprv	Goal Align	Pay Equity	Entrepreneurial Workplace
Wage/Salary					
Profit Sharing			✓		
Gainsharing		✓	✓		
Piece-rate/Comm.	✓	✓		✓	
Total Perf. System	✓	✓	✓	✓	✓

The wage-and-salary system meets none of these objectives. Profit sharing can align employee and organizational goals. However, this is likely true for all employees only in small organizations, and for the executive group only in larger organizations. The question arises, why do companies continue to use conventional wage-and-salary systems in combination with annual profit sharing? In my work with owners and managers across the country, I find the following reasons the most often cited for maintaining the status quo.

"We've always done it this way."   Simple inertia explains many organizations' unwillingness to look at alternative pay and performance management systems. The current system of fixed, guaranteed pay, coupled with aversive management by exception, does work in a limited way. The low performance and lack of employee initiative and creativity produced by this system has come to be an expectation of management. Consequently, it is often difficult for them to imagine employees performing differently.

"Pay-for-performance is too much trouble."   There is no question that a pay-for-performance system requires more effort than simply maintaining the existing system. The new system has to be installed and communicated. Managers have to change the way they supervise. Performance data has to be collected. The decision to convert will depend upon how important the five performance pay system goals are to the organization's success.

"I'll lose control of my employees."   Yes, and it's about time. Directly linking pay to objective performance outcomes removes the "middle man." The manager role shifts from direct supervision to serving as a liaison between the external marketplace and the employee group, and becoming a resource to assist employees in maximizing their performance and earnings.

"Workers want guaranteed pay."   My experience has been that initially workers are apprehensive about the conversion. However, once the conversion to pay-for-performance is made, the workers adapt most readily and are quite resistant

to any effort to remove the system later. It is most often management and ownership that have problems adjusting to the system.

Many companies meet resistance from employees when pay-for-performance is proposed. Often this is because the upside potential of the performance pay system does not compensate for the downside risk. Several years ago I was meeting with a prospective company to install an organization-wide performance pay system. On my second visit the meeting began with the CEO telling me excitedly that they had discovered a flaw in performance pay through their own independent research. They had surveyed their employees and asked them, "Would you rather receive a five percent base pay increase or have the opportunity to earn five percent of your base pay through a performance pay system?"

The response was overwhelmingly in favor of the base pay increase. I was briefly dumbstruck. I then said, "What you have asked is, would you rather have some money, or maybe have some money?" Given the question, the upside potential earnings were no more than the downside risk. Two questions should have been asked instead. First, "Would you rather have a five percent increase or a fifteen percent upside earnings potential?" Second, "Would you like to have a five percent base pay increase now, and risk a five percent of the work force layoff when profits decline?"

"*Workers aren't smart enough to live on variable pay.*" Executives of companies that are seasonal or cyclical in their profits are concerned that employees will not save during the peak season and will get into financial trouble during the down season. It is interesting to note that prior to the industrial revolution some 75 percent of the work force was self-

101

employed, primarily as farmers. The view that pay is fixed is a relatively new one in the history of work. In any event, it is simply not true that in this age of credit cards and quick loans employees always live within their means even in a fixed pay system.

Given the fact that many employees today have never functioned in a variable pay system, it is a good idea to provide some training and advice on how to budget under variable pay. Further, the company must share profit projections with its employees to enable them to plan. Some organizations try to minimize the effects of business cycles by adjusting goals and payout requirements to level the payouts. I strongly discourage this practice. "Smoothing" the business cycles will not align employee and organizational objectives. Further, the company will pay out in periods when it is unaffordable.

"Employees will quit during bad times." A very common concern is that employees will only stay with the company as long as their pay is at, or above, market pay. As soon as pay falls below market, they will quit the company and seek employment elsewhere. This concern assumes employees are unable to adopt an entrepreneurial outlook. The employee must decide whether the opportunity for unlimited future earnings outweighs any short-term pay reduction.

This decision rests on the employee's faith in the organization's ability to reverse a business downturn. Good communications regarding organizational strategies and projections are critical for employees to make the best decision. Further, a history must be in place in which the company has lived up to its word and, in fact, shared gains with employees. But what if the projections for the next several years are bad? Then employees will leave of their own volition in a variable pay system or be forced out by layoffs in a conventional, fixed-pay system.

Many business pundits tell us that the days of long-term loyal employees are over. The new employee will hop from job to job as opportunities arise. If we retain the conventional pay system, with its limited pay opportunity and repeated layoffs, this forecast is likely true. But what if we moved toward pay-for-performance? The better the company does, the better the employee does. In theory, there is no upper limit on an employee's pay, except the ability of the total organization to grow.

Pay-for-performance is, in fact, the only means by which a poorly educated employee will ever share in the American dream. The conventional system caps this individual's pay at a very modest wage. In pay-for-performance the employee's earnings rise continually with the organization's long-term success.

Linking pay to organizational profitability also benefits employees who are currently working in piece-rate or sales commission plans. On commission, a salesperson must sell more each succeeding year to earn more. When the commission rate (or piece-rate) is linked to overall organizational profits, the commission rate increases automatically as the company prospers. The result is that the same level of production provides increased earnings. In effect, the employee's efforts have created a residual or equity position.

"We won't be able to hire anyone." An employee interviews with your company. The job she is applying for pays $25,000 in the local market. She is told, "We pay a base salary of $20,000 but if the company is successful this year and

103

you perform well, you could earn up to $35,000. Last year's average earnings of employees in the job you are applying for were $30,000."

If the employee chooses another company that offers a guaranteed salary, you should ask the question, "What have we really lost?" Pay-for-performance attracts a different type of employee to your organization. These employees are risk-takers and confident in their abilities and in your organization. Is this not the type of employee group that will help a company prosper? The key to successful recruitment in a pay-for-performance organization is developing a good track record that proves the company will honor its commitment to pay-for-performance.

References

[1] *The Hay Report: Compensation and Benefits Strategies for 1995 and Beyond*. Philadelphia: The Hay Group, 1994.

[2] Alan S. Binder (Ed.). *Paying for Productivity: A Look at the Evidence.* Washington, D.C: The Brookings Institution, 1990.

Chapter 10: The Total Performance System Perspective

THE TOTAL PERFORMANCE SYSTEM APPROACH TO MANAGEMENT IS CONTRASTED WITH THE INDUSTRIAL HUMANIST MANAGEMENT THEORY. THE TOTAL PERFORMANCE SYSTEM IS DESCRIBED AS HAVING COMPONENTS WHICH INCLUDE THE PERFORMANCE SCORECARD, PROFIT- INDEXED PERFORMANCE PAY, AND POSITIVE LEADERSHIP.

My first project as a psychologist was working in a large psychiatric hospital in the Midwest. The patient I was assigned was labeled a "paranoid schizophrenic." He had been in the hospital many years and spent most of his day yelling in a gravel-like voice about various plots against him or, alternatively, his daughter's loose morals. The day I arrived, "Mr. Jones" was on everybody's blacklist. They had just returned from an outing to a local air base and Mr. Jone's yelling had cut short the trip.

Over the years, Mr. Jones had been exposed to "talking therapies," electroconvulsive shock, and a regimen of drugs that he was presently taking. None of these had been effective. The likelihood of Mr. Jones successfully interviewing for a job was near zero. He was doomed to remain in the hospital permanently. My training was in behavior modification, the application of B.F. Skinner's theory of positive reinforcement. Given this orientation, my approach to helping Mr. Jones was to pay him to stop yelling (technically, positive reinforcement). Since I could not use money, the pay consisted of tokens redeemable at the hospital store and cigarettes (a payment that was socially acceptable in the 70s).

The "therapy" plan was straightforward. Mr. Jones would sit in a room off the ward. In the early sessions, if he talked in a normal tone of voice for one minute, he received a reward.

What he said was not considered, only the way it was said. If he received three consecutive rewards, the time requirement was increased by one minute. The results were nothing short of phenomenal. Within two weeks he was consistently talking in a normal tone of voice for four hours. This had not occurred in over twelve years in the hospital, even under heavy sedation.

I was quite pleased with myself. My first project had been an unqualified success. Not only had Mr. Jones stopped yelling, but in addition, the staff informed me that he actually looked forward to our sessions. However, my self-congratulations were short-lived. Over the next several weeks it became apparent that Mr. Jones stopped yelling only during our sessions. As soon as I left the ward he started up again. Given this, to get him out of the hospital I would have had to follow him around with a carton of cigarettes the rest of his life!

In thinking through this situation, I arrived at a view that is the basis of this book and the Total Performance System, to be described next. I asked myself why Mr. Jones was yelling when it was clear he could control it. With this new set of questions, I began to look at the *system* in which he lived. The hospital provided Mr. Jones a place to live and three meals a day. There were regular movies, a nine-hole golf course, and an Olympic-size swimming pool. Further, Mr. Jones' family received substantial disability payments for his "condition" because it was war-related. These benefits were all tied to Mr. Jones' yelling since he had no other serious medical condition. If he stopped yelling, his family would lose the disability payments and he would be put out on the street. Given this system, he would have been crazy to stop screaming!

The noted psychiatrist R.D. Laing told us that there are no crazy people, only crazy systems. People adapt as best they can to the systems in which they find themselves. Crazy systems, like cults, foster what others would view as crazy behavior. We are exposed to many and various systems. The most prevalent of these systems are the family, the school, the church, our circle of friends, the community, and the workplace.

The moment-to-moment interactions in these systems are subtle and complex. These interactions are further complicated through their interplay with our personal genetics and experiences. The permutation of possible outcomes reaches into the millions at any given point in time. Trying to precisely predict a specific outcome in these complex systems is somewhat analogous to a physicist trying to tell us where a leaf will fall on a windy day.

Despite this complexity, within a specific system over time, people adopt behavioral strategies that generally prove to be the most successful for them given their unique personal histories. Just as the physicist can't tell us exactly where the leaf will fall, he can tell us it will fall down and on the side away from the wind.

It is most difficult for an individual to operate effectively in unstable systems since the rules of the game continually change. This inability to determine how the system operates not only reduces effectiveness, but also can be very unsettling for an individual. Employees in organizational systems that fail to provide objective goals and frequent performance feedback are akin to the leaf in the windstorm.

The Total Performance System approach to understanding human behavior has many critics. The chief criticism is that it conflicts with views that place the locus of control "in the person" rather than "in the system." This controversy is largely due to misunderstandings about the nature of systems control and personal choice. Gilbert Ryle, the philosopher, described the relationship this way. Suppose an invisible being from another planet appeared at a chess match. The being observed two people playing chess for several hours. When the game was over, the being materialized and spoke to the players. "You people are nothing but slaves to your game. Every move you make is predetermined by the rules of the game." The players respond, "It is true that every move is determined by the rules of the game. But how we play the game is completely up to us and is never the same for any two games." [1]

Each system we find ourselves in has its set of rules. We may play the game any way we wish. However, if we don't understand the rules, or violate the rules, we will be unsuccessful at the game. A system we find ourselves in for one-third of our adult lives is the workplace. Each workplace has its rules, and the employees who succeed at the "game" of work are those who play the best within these rules.

Three Strategies for Optimizing Employee Performance. To optimize employee performance, management has three strategies available: hire good people, exercise strong leadership, or create a Total Performance System. Two of these strategies — hiring good people and leadership — are traditional strategies, while the creation of a behavioral system is less conventional.

1) Hire Good People. A frequent complaint of managers is, "If only I had good people, I could get the job done." If employees were motivated, creative, skilled, and productive, the work would be accomplished. The secret, then, is to recruit and hire only these kinds of employees. Unfortunately, there are two major obstacles to hiring good people. First, the technology available for selecting high-quality employees is still relatively primitive. Resumes, interviews, tests, and references are the chief selection tools and too often prove themselves unreliable. The research on the predictive validity of these tools is also discouraging.

A more serious problem is that this view is basically illogical. The underlying assumption is that people will perform in the recruiting organization the same way as they have in other organizations, or in the same way as they perform in an interview or test. This view assumes that human behavior is constant across different situations, when casual observation tells us otherwise. A person acts differently in different situations. We don't behave the same at work as we do at home, at church, or at a social outing. We behave appropriate to the setting. A person who is successful in adjusting his behavior to different situations is said to be "well adjusted." A person who doesn't adjust appropriately is said to be "maladjusted."

An organization with high employee turnover may be ineffective in its selection process, but the source of the problem is much more likely to be that the organization's management system relies on coercion. Placing the accountability solely with employees may make management feel good, but it does little to solve the problem. Sitting in the faculty lounge when I was a teacher, I often overheard the comment, "If I only had good students I could teach." I thought, "If we only had good students we wouldn't need teachers." In any event, whether we attribute the problem of poor performance to the employee or to the organization's performance system, the only practical solution is to improve the system, since there is little we can do to guarantee we will only select good employees.

I should add that this conclusion in no way means we should quit holding employees accountable for their performances simply because our organization may lack a well-engineered performance system. Regardless of the quality of the system, employees who fail to contribute to the organization must be replaced. To argue it's not their fault would be equivalent to passing out medical licenses to untrained doctors because the school's curriculum wasn't perfected. The argument presented here is that simply blaming employees, or fiddling with the selection process, won't solve the problem. We must reengineer the system to improve employee performance.

2) Leadership. A second strategy for ensuring high performing employees is through dynamic, charismatic leadership. There is little doubt that good leadership will usually improve subordinate performance. But leadership is, after all, simply another set of behaviors. Good leadership can only be maintained in an organization whose performance system supports it. Whether good leaders are made or born, it is clear that a punitive, inequitable, unpredictable performance system can unmake them. The leadership style in an organization is no better than the style of the next management level.

Even if leadership is supported by an organization, it is risky to rely solely on charismatic leadership to ensure high employee performance. Leaders come and go, or their personalities may change over time. A well-engineered performance system is not dependent upon any one individual.

Feels like it is (handwritten annotation)

Further, because a performance system does not rely on any one person, it supports a "flat" organization which in turn reduces payroll expense and increases organizational responsiveness and flexibility.

In his book *The E-Myth Revisited* [2], Michael Gerber points out that entrepreneurs often construct ineffective performance systems because they lack the temperament, experience, time, or technical expertise to design effective ones. I would add to this that entrepreneurs are often "doers" who are reluctant to delegate responsibilities and, therefore, tend to create autocratic management systems. I have seen entrepreneurs create organizations they would personally never work in, or if they did, would likely find themselves fired.

Conventional Pay and Industrial Humanism. Ensuring high performance employees through hiring and firing or leadership has been the conventional wisdom for many years, and has served its function in the absence of better alternatives. Behavioral research over the past fifty years shows us another way. Just as you can still get from here to there on horseback, you could continue to use traditional management strategies — but there is a better way. *How to get here?* (handwritten annotation)

The components of an organization's performance system are its selection, training, supervision, appraisal, promotion, and compensation practices. Surprisingly, of these components, compensation practices are the most out of touch with performance systems theory.

111

The perseverance of the conventional pay system is explained well enough by the fact that it is familiar, easy, and natural. However, there are additional reasons for its continuance. Most business people are somewhat familiar with the theories spawned by the Hawthorne Electric studies in the 1950s. The management theories collectively termed *Industrial Humanism* particularly flourished in the 1960s. Some of its better known proponents were Abraham Maslow and his "hierarchy of needs," Chris Argyris and job enrichment, and McGregor's "theory X and theory Y." These theories are still today the mainstay of management theory in business and personnel courses.

In brief, the industrial humanists argued that employee performance is a function of personal and social factors more so than pay. People perform best when they are given interesting and meaningful work, and a positive social environment with their supervisors and coworkers.

Since the social environment was the determinant of employee performance, the solutions were directed at its improvement. Thus, American management was exposed at various times to job enrichment, sensitivity training, quality circles, and other strategies to improve the meaningfulness of jobs and social relations. The results were notably unimpressive and one hears little about these programs today. But the basic premise that, the means to achieve employee performance are improvements in social relations and job enrichment, have not gone away. They keep resurfacing under different names. Today, most organizations aren't enriching jobs, they are "reengineering." They don't conduct quality circles any more, they have "self-directed work teams." The idea of allowing employees to meet and discuss solutions to work problems can't be argued against. Similarly, jobs can certainly be too narrowly defined. But the fundamental performance system is still ignored.

We keep rearranging the furniture on a sinking ship! We still pay for time, which is directly counter to improving productivity. We still pay everyone in a given job about the same, which is unfair and discourages high performers. We still manage by perception and exception, which suppresses employee initiative and creativity and depresses performance. We still pay employees independent of company profitability, which makes adversaries of ownership, management, and workers. We still provide entitlement annual increases, which artificially holds down the wages of good performers and puts job security at risk. We still make it a practice to promote good performers to management which makes producers become nonproducers, and creates a bloated management bureaucracy. We must change our pay system.

Not only has management bought into the "humanist" view of what makes an organization work, so have employees. Today's "entitlement" society has developed parallel to humanist management thinking. People deserve a good living irrespective of what they do. Employees are entitled to a paycheck if they meet the bare minimum of job requirements, and regardless of the profitability of the company that employs them.

It is the height of irony that as the world moves rapidly toward free market enterprise, the U.S. plunges headlong toward the failed economic philosophy of socialism. It is my belief that conventional entitlement pay has been a major contributor to the demise of the entrepreneurial spirit and work ethic in America. Perhaps no owner or manager of a

113

business can solve the country's crisis, but they can change their own organizations to reflect what has worked best for America and its people.

It's not so much that people are greedy and must have more and more money. Rather, we are naturally engineered to explore our environment to seek out rewards and avoid punishers. We need to experience some control over our environment. We need a "scorecard." In business, the company's scorecard is profit. For the employee, it is pay.

When pay is artificially disconnected from performance, people seek out other scorecards. When I was a college professor, there was little connection between performance and pay. As a result, the faculty sought out other scorecards such as titles, the best offices, status committee assignments, leadership roles, and others. Many theorists argue that rewards should be "intrinsic" to the work. In some occupations this may be true. For example, authors, musicians, artists, research scientists, developmental programmers, and others engage in jobs that have natural rewards built into them. But even these individuals are concerned with "extrinsic" equity in terms of peer and public recognition and pay. However, the great majority of jobs offers little in the way of intrinsic rewards. Try telling an assembly-line worker or clerk their jobs should be intrinsically motivating.

3) The Performance System Perspective. On a summer morning, a farmer rises early to harvest his crop. Next, he transports the crop to a local storage facility. The storage facility then arranges to transport its produce via rail to a processing plant. The processing plant sells its product to a wholesaler, who in turn sells and delivers the product to a retailer, who then sells the product to the consumer. Who is

114

managing this system? Ultimately, the consumer, but moment-to-moment, no one — it is self-managed by the individual parties in their own interests.

Biological, ecological, economic, social, and business systems all have in common this self-regulating characteristic. The concept that a system can be self-regulating is difficult for many of us to accept. We think in direct cause and effect terms. We want to believe there is a "power behind the throne," or someone who is "pulling the strings." We want things planned — not random. Few of us have caught up with, or fully understand, the shift in theoretical physics from Newtonian cause and effect thinking to modern complexity theory.

We want to believe that our government is managing the "system." But, in fact, our economy is largely self-regulated. Government can certainly affect the system through laws, taxation, and spending but often the outcomes are contrary to the objectives. Governmental controls are only one of a myriad of variables that operate within our economy. Still, it is common to ascribe a good or poor economy to Washington. We vote in or out those politicians who, largely by accident, coincide with positive and negative economic cycles.

Where governments have tried to directly control large, complex systems, they have eventually failed. After communism fell in Poland a friend of mine who had left the country returned to visit. He decided to travel across the country by train. When he asked the price of a luxury sleeper car for a five-day trip the reply was ninety-five dollars. My friend was incredulous. This price couldn't be right. He assumed the agent was incorrectly converting the currencies and asked to see the price schedule. To his surprise, the price quoted by the agent was correct. Glancing further down the price sheet he noticed the price sheet had not been revised since 1954! The central planning price committee must have forgotten to meet!

Central planning failed in the Soviet Union and elsewhere. When we have tried price controls or other major interventions, they have not worked well here. The current crusade is to "devolve" government from Washington back to the states and local communities. This objective is a recognition of the inability of a few people to effectively manage a complex system. There is a parallel within an organization. Management can attempt its own version of "central planning" and employ traditional command-and-control supervision to ensure that its plans are carried out. As the system grows larger and more complex, however, this approach will ultimately fail.

10.5

The alternative is to structure a performance system within the organization that eliminates the need for centralized command and control. The question arises, why must we design a system for an organization when such systems occur naturally elsewhere? There are two reasons.

First, the conventional organization has artificially severed the connection between the customer and the financial success of the employee. A self-employed person's self-interests are directly related to the customer's willingness to purchase a product or service. In the wage-and-salary system, this is most often not the case. As organizations have grown larger and more complex, many job functions have been removed from a direct relationship with the customer.

Second, in today's competitive world a successful organization must be improvement-oriented. It must continuously enhance and expand its products and services, while at the same time improve productivity and quality. In the conventional system, the value of these improvements has not been passed down to the employee.

A performance system would reestablish the relationship between employees and the external marketplace by linking pay to the organization's profits. In a small organization in which all employees interact with customers, this linkage might be all that is required to align employee and customer interests and to develop a continuous improvement philosophy. In larger, more complex organizations, the system would require additional linkages between job results and profits. These linkages are provided by personal, team, and departmental *Performance Scorecards.*

The Total Performance System. In working with all sorts of organizations, we experimented with many types of performance improvement and performance pay systems including commission and piece-rate plans, gainshare plans, standard time plans, performance credit plans, and goal-driven plans. Some of these plans relied upon supervisor feedback only; others were linked to recognition programs, merchandise programs, time off, and money. Each combination proved incomplete in some way.

In the mid-1980s, we began to measure performance using the Performance Scorecard. Shortly thereafter, we linked scorecard performance to organizational profit to create a performance pay system. In the 1990s, this system was

linked

117

reinforced with Positive Leadership training for managers. The result of this evolution is the *Total Performance System.*

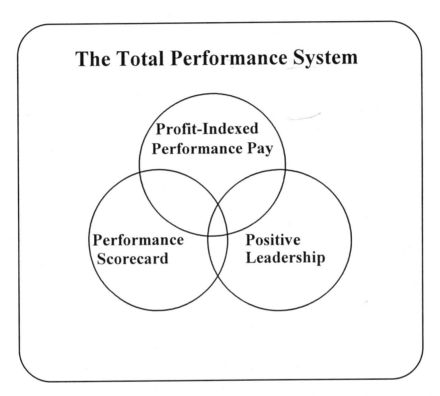

The Total Performance System

Profit-Indexed
Performance Pay

Performance
Scorecard

Positive
Leadership

The *Total Performance System* (TPS) is an integrated, organization-wide pay and management system. TPS is a proven alternative to conventional entitlement pay and the practices of management by perception and exception. TPS consists of three components: the Performance Scorecard, Profit-Indexed Performance Pay, and Positive Leadership.

The Performance Scorecard. The core of the system is the Performance Scorecard. The Performance Scorecard provides a universal format for objective performance measurement across an organization. The scorecard *balances* and

10.6

prioritizes performance objectives at each organizational level. The scorecard compares performance to both a base and goal to compute a dynamic *percent gain* that focuses the organization on continuous, incremental improvement rather than absolute goals.

The scorecard converts performances across functions to a common scale that ensures performance pay *equity* among job positions. Through the measurement design strategy of *cascading objectives,* each scorecard is linked to the next organizational level to create a common focus across the organization toward its key objectives. The performance scorecard will be described in Chapter 11.

Profit-Indexed Performance Pay. The second component of the *Total Performance System* is Profit-Indexed Performance Pay (PIPP). Monthly performance pay opportunity is determined by the organization's or division's *controllable net income.* How much of the opportunity an employee earns is determined by his performance on the performance scorecard. An employee's performance pay opportunity is increased annually instead of the wage or salary. Profit-Indexed Performance Pay will be described in Chapter 12.

Positive Leadership. The third component of the *Total Performance System* is Positive Leadership. Positive Leadership consists of three management skill sets: performance analysis, performance improvement, and performance coaching.

Performance Analysis teaches managers and supervisors how to objectively measure performance, how to evaluate performance trends, and how to analyze both interdepartmental and process-level activity to pinpoint improvement opportunities.

119

Performance Improvement refers to strategies for improving performance once opportunities have been pinpointed. Examples of these strategies are work flow improvement, work scheduling and work distribution, cross-training, process training, precision feedback systems, and others.

Performance Coaching is a change in the role of the manager from management by perception to empirical management, and from management by exception to management of incremental improvement. Further, the manager role shifts from traditional command and control to a support function in which the manager becomes more a facilitator than a supervisor. Positive Leadership is described in Chapter 13.

Design, Implementation, and Transition Strategies. Chapter 14 outlines strategies and tactics for developing and managing the *Total Performance System.* These strategies were developed through hundreds of applications and ensure an organization can design and implement TPS efficiently and effectively and manage the system over time.

References

[1] Gilbert Ryle. *The Concept of Mind.* Chicago: The University of Chicago Press, 1949.

[2] Michael E. Gerber. *The E-Myth Revisited.* New York: HarperCollins, 1995.

Chapter 11:
The Performance Scorecard

THE PERFORMANCE SCORECARD IS EXPLAINED AND HOW CASCADING OBJECTIVES ARE USED TO DESIGN AN INTEGRATED ORGANIZATION-WIDE SCORECARD SYSTEM.

The Performance Scorecard. The Performance Scorecard was introduced in the 1980s by Felix and Riggs at the University of Oregon Productivity Center[1]. Their term for this approach to performance measurement was the "performance matrix." The Performance Scorecard is essentially a conversion table that allows several performance measures to be included in the computation of an overall performance index.

I have described how to develop these scorecards in two previous books: *Designing and Managing an Organization-Wide Incentive Pay System*, 1990[2] and *How to Design Effective Incentive Plans*, 1993,[3]. The reader is referred to these sources for a detailed discussion of the design of Performance Scorecards. The following examples describe the components of the Performance Scorecard.

121

Performance Scorecard

Performance Scales

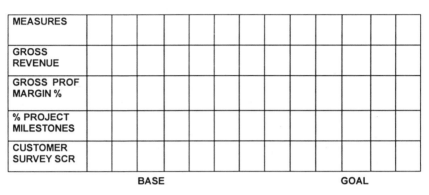

MEASURES															
GROSS REVENUE															
GROSS PROF MARGIN %															
% PROJECT MILESTONES															
CUSTOMER SURVEY SCR															

BASE   GOAL

The *performance measures* are listed on the left. A well-designed scorecard will contain two to six such measures that are aligned with the organization's objectives. The scorecard measures should be directly influenced by the employees to whom they are assigned and should refer to objective outcomes rather than subjective perceptions.

In this example, the scorecard is for a sales manager and the measures are gross revenue, gross profit margin percentage, percent project milestones met, and the average salesperson's rating on a customer survey. The project milestones measure rewards completion of a project assigned to the sales manager.

Performance Scorecard

Performance Scales

MEASURES	-20	-10	0	10	20	30	40	50	60	80	100		
GROSS REVENUE (000)	10	15	20	25	30	35	40	45	50	55	60		
GROSS PROF MARGIN %	20	22	24	26	28	30	32	34	36	38	40		
% PROJECT MILESTONES	50	55	60	65	70	75	80	85	90	95	100		
CUSTOMER SURVEY SCR	4.0	4.5	5.0	5.5	6.0	6.5	7.0	7.5	8.0	8.5	9.0		

BASE   GOAL

To the right of the measure is the ***performance scale***. Each measure's unique scale converts to the upper common scale to allow a single performance index to be computed. To design a measure's scale, the two end points, or base and goal, must first be determined.

The ***base*** is set at, or somewhat below, current performance levels. This practice ensures that employees immediately participate in the performance pay system in at least a small way. If bases are set above current performance levels, performance improvement will often occur much more slowly. The ***goal*** is the performance level required for the employee to receive the maximum performance payment for the measure. Goals are set by determining the performance level required for the organizational scorecard to meet its goal.

The common scale intervals increase in ten percent increments except near goal, where the final two intervals increase in twenty percent increments. This acceleration in payout is in recognition of the fact that incremental performance improvements are usually more difficult near goal than right above base. Two negative intervals below base are included in each measure's scale. These negative intervals are designed to ensure balanced performance by preventing employees from ignoring all but one measure to guarantee a partial payout.

Performance Scorecard

Performance Scales

MEASURES	-20	-10	0	10	20	30	40	50	60	80	100	WGT	
GROSS REVENUE (000)	10	15	20	25	30	35	40	45	50	55	60	.20	
GROSS PROF MARGIN %	20	22	24	26	28	30	32	34	36	38	40	.20	
% PROJECT MILESTONES	50	55	60	65	70	75	80	85	90	95	100	.40	
CUSTOMER SURVEY SCR	4.0	4.5	5.0	5.5	6.0	6.5	7.0	7.5	8.0	8.5	9.0	.20	
			BASE								GOAL		

124

Finally, each measure is assigned a *priority weight.* These priority weights define the percentage of the total performance index and performance pay payout each measure determines. The priority weights sum to 100 percent. The priority weights in a given scorecard should match the priorities assigned in the overall organizational scorecard which will be described next. In cases where a scorecard does not include measures related to all of the organizational scorecard measures, the proportions should still remain equivalent to the organizational scorecard to ensure total alignment across all scorecards.

Performance Scorecard

Performance Scales

MEASURES	-20	-10	0	10	20	30	40	50	60	80	100	WGT	SCR
GROSS REVENUE (000)	10	15	20	25	30	35	40	45	50	55	60	.20	-4
GROSS PROF MARGIN %	20	22	24	26	28	30	32	34	36	38	40	.20	0
% PROJECT MILESTONES	50	55	60	65	70	75	80	85	90	95	100	.40	20
CUSTOMER SURVEY SCR	4.0	4.5	5.0	5.5	6.0	6.5	7.0	7.5	8.0	8.5	9.0	.20	20

BASE   GOAL

36

Performance Index

125

The *actual performance* interval attained is underlined in the example. To compute the performance index, the common scale interval that the actual performance falls into is identified. This interval's scale percentage is multiplied by the measure's weight to compute the measure's *weighted score*. The scores for all the measures are summed to compute the overall scorecard *performance index*.

11.2 For example, on the sample scorecard "gross revenue" actual performance for the month is $10,000. This result falls in the -20 percent interval. The weight for this measure is 20 percent. Multiplying, the weighted percent gain for this measure is -20 x 20% or -4%. The remaining measure calculations are performed in the same manner.

Percent Gain Formula. An alternative to the scale approach is to compute the actual percent gain of each measure using the formula (actual minus base) divided by the (goal minus base). The advantage to this approach is there is no "rounding" of actual performance within an interval. The disadvantages are that the "look-up" feature of the interval table is replaced by a calculation which makes the score more difficult to derive.

The interval approach also allows the developer to adjust the scale intervals in a nonlinear fashion to reflect the actual difficulty associated with performance improvements across the scale. For example, to encourage new behaviors, the scale intervals could be small immediately above base and larger as performance reaches goal. Or, for existing behaviors, as in the example, the reverse could be applied in which the intervals are smaller as performance approaches the goal.

Performance Caps. The reader will notice that the scales "cap" performances both above goal and below base. Performance on a given measure cannot exceed 100 percent of goal or fall below -20 percent. Performances above goal, then, are not rewarded more than performance at goal. There is no recognition or payment for above-goal performance on the scorecard.

This drawback is a compromise. If the caps are removed, the scorecard is no longer balanced. Employees could focus on one measure and drive it well above goal. In an uncapped scorecard this would enable these employees to perform poorly on other measures and still receive 100 percent of the performance pay payout for an unbalanced performance. Assuming each measure in the scorecard is aligned with the organization's overall objectives, this unbalanced performance would not meet the total organization's needs.

Second, allowing the scorecard measures to exceed 100 percent of goal could produce a performance index in excess of 100 percent. The performance pay payout to the employees receiving this index would then be more than 100 percent of the opportunity. The result would be that the funding share percentage would exceed the original requirements (the system would overpay employees).

It can be argued that for employees in job positions that directly affect the funding formula, this is less of a problem. An example is a revenue measure in a sales position scorecard. However, the problem of the scorecard becoming unbalanced would still be an issue. A third solution is to track such measures as a three month rolling average which will credit above-goal performance in the following two months.

Adjusting Bases and Goals for Performance Improvements. Our solution to the general issue of performances improving beyond the original goal is to review all performances at six-month intervals in the beginning of the system, and annually when the system is "mature." If performances across several scorecards related to a given organizational objective are consistently above the goal (with no detriment to other performance objectives), then the organization goal and all related sub-scorecard goals should be adjusted.

When performance goals are increased in this manner, the Performance Pay Multiplier should increase also, which will adjust the payouts so that they are approximately comparable. If not, performance pay opportunity should be increased to prevent the problem of asking for more and more, for the same payout. The opportunity adjustments could be applied to specific sets of scorecards by increasing the performance pay bases, or across the organization by increasing the range of the performance pay multiplier.

Adjusting for Variations in the Opportunity to Perform. Some performance measures' opportunity to perform vary substantially from month to month because of factors largely outside the control of the employees. The result is that in one month the employees may achieve 150 percent of goal, while in the next month the opportunity is limited to 50 percent of goal regardless of how well employees perform. There are four solutions to this problem.

First, the best solution is to make no adjustment at all! If you adjust goals to ensure an equal opportunity, then you are artificially separating the employee from the organization, which will cause alignment problems. If you must adjust, the goal can be adjusted each month or quarter, in advance, to better match opportunity. Third, a moving average can be applied to performance to smooth out variations in opportunity. Fourth, the organization can redesign the job, cross-train, or install flexible work scheduling to provide more consistent performance opportunities. This alternative is ultimately the best long-term solution for the organization.

The key features of the Performance Scorecard are:

1) The scorecards are a performance improvement tool. The Performance Scorecard provides each employee specific, objective goals to work toward, and monthly feedback on progress toward those goals. This combination of precise objectives and monthly feedback is the engine of performance improvement.

2) The scorecards align employee performance goals with the organization's. Each scorecard measure is developed using the "cascading objectives" method to be described next. The result is that each measure aligns with the next organizational level and, ultimately, with the overall organization's goals.

3) The scorecards ensure balanced performance. Each scorecard is designed to track both production and quality, as well as performances that affect long-term profitability.

4) The scorecards facilitate cooperation. For organizations that install personal scorecards, each scorecard includes one or more departmental or team measures in addition to the personal measures. Interdepartmental cooperation is fostered through "linked" scorecard measures where a support, or upstream, department is partly rewarded on the performance of the supported, or downstream, departments.

5) The scorecards are a management information tool. An organization-wide Performance Scorecard system provides each management level a precise and timely tool for pin-pointing performance improvement opportunities and determining the specific causes of organizational successes and problems.

6) The scorecards are a performance management tool. Each manager receives a monthly scorecard for each of their direct reports. These scorecards replace conventional management by perception and exception, and enable the manager to coach and support incremental, month-to-month performance improvement.

7) The scorecards foster an entrepreneurial workplace. As described earlier, management by perception and exception creates a reactive, uncreative employee group. The introduction of Performance Scorecards allows employees to work toward a goal rather than simply avoid making mistakes. Further, profit-indexed pay makes true partners of all employees in the organization, who now have a personal stake in the organization's long-term success.

1.5 **Cascading Objectives Design Method.** The Cascading Objectives method is used to develop an organization's scorecards. This method ensures each scorecard drives the overall corporate objectives and also greatly increases the efficiency of the design process. The process is to first design the organizational scorecard, and then scorecards for the division, department, and so on, down to each unique job position.

The organizational scorecard is critical to the success of the overall system, since each subordinate scorecard is designed to align with the measures and priority weights of this scorecard. The following is a general diagram of the key objectives for most businesses.

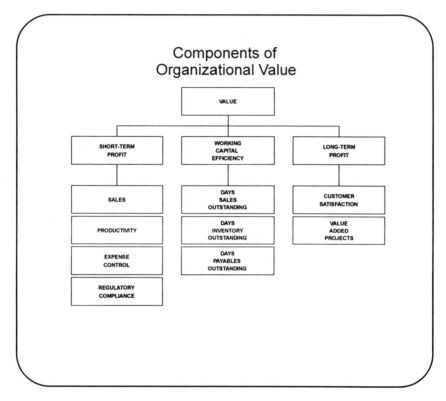

Organizational Value. The value of an organization can be thought of as its current profitability, its working capital efficiency, and its long-term profit position with respect to customer satisfaction and value-added projects.

Short-Term Profit. To make a profit you have to sell something, keep expenses down, and try to stay out of jail! Current sales, productivity (labor cost), expenses, and regulatory

131

compliance determine short-term profits. Labor expense is separated from all other expenses because it is addressed differently in a *Total Performance System*. Regulatory compliance refers to employee behaviors that are regulated by the government such as safety, environment, and personnel laws.

Working Capital Efficiency. This category refers to employee performances that affect the balance sheet or cash flow of the organization. Two measures of this category are:

$$\text{Current Ratio} = \frac{\text{Cash} + \text{Accounts Receivable} + \text{Inventory}}{\text{Current Liabilities}}$$

Days Out = DSO + DIO - DPO

where DSO is days sales outstanding, DIO is days inventory outstanding, and DPO is days payables outstanding.

Long-Term Profitability. In addition to short-term profitability, the organizational scorecard should include measures that have deferred outcomes. The two subcategories here are employee performances that affect customer satisfaction, and projects that will have a positive impact upon profitability in the future.

The top three objectives, short-term profit, working capital efficiency, and long-term profit, make up the organizational scorecard. Each organization will define these categories to meet its unique objectives. However, it is critical that the scorecard not become cluttered with too many measures. The "Top 50 Priorities" is an oxymoron. An organizational scorecard with more than six measures may be the result of defining a profit multiplier that covers too large and complex an organization, including measures that are more

132

appropriate at a lower organizational level, or confusing means with ends.

Measuring Project Performances. Value-added project measures can be organized under one project credit system. Each project is first assigned a credit value using the "nominal group technique," or other of several well-established methods, for determining relative staff requirements among several projects. Once staff days are assigned to each project, milestones are defined that preferably occur monthly, but not less than quarterly. Quality and completeness criteria are defined for each milestone. The project's total staff days are then allocated across the milestones, based upon how important they are and their duration.

Each month, the staff days associated with milestones completed to criteria are awarded to the project person or team. These earned days are compared to a monthly *earned days* goal on the Performance Scorecard. For example, suppose a project team had three projects assigned and each project had three milestones. The available credit might look like:

Project	Total Staff Days	MS 1	MS2	MS3
A	10	3	3	4
B	25	10	10	5
C	15	5	5	5

If, in the month, the team completed project A's first milestone and B's second milestone, they would earn 3 + 10 or 13 days. If the Performance Scorecard base were 5 days and the goal was 15 days, they would receive a score of (13-5)/(15-5) or 80%. Or, the project milestones can be set up as percent of deadlines met on sub-scorecards. Each milestone would

133

have a due date and a weight. The percent due date met would be computed and compared to the scorecard scale for the project or milestone. The percent due date formula is (date completed - date assigned)/(date due - date assigned)

	-20	-10	00	10	20	30	40	50	60	80	100	WGT	SCR
P1	50	55	<u>60</u>	65	70	75	80	85	90	95	100	30	0
P2	50	55	60	65	70	75	80	85	<u>90</u>	95	100	20	12
P3	50	55	60	65	70	75	80	85	90	95	<u>100</u>	50	50

Performance Index = 62%

All projects could be rolled into a master long-term profit improvement project scorecard. This master scorecard performance index would then be rolled into the organizational scorecard.

Value-Added Predictor Measures. An example of a predictor measure might be market penetration or sales prospecting performance as a predictor of future revenue. For customer service a predictor measure might be the percent of employees completing a training program, or an improvement in a targeted service measure like turnaround time. A productivity predictor might be the percent of employees cross-trained or enrolled in a flexible scheduling system. Expense reduction predictors might be the number of process improvement projects submitted by employee teams, etc. Another alternative might be to set sub-goals that move toward the ultimate long-term profit goal across the span of the project or longer.

Measuring Social Responsibility. The concept of social responsibility covers a very broad set of issues. For convenience, it can be divided into responsibility toward employees and responsibility toward the community. Employee indicators could be turnover statistics, grievances, or employee surveys. Community indicators could be surveys, percent of employees involved in community work, or the number of commendations from the public. Responsibility to the community could also be measured as the completion of projects aimed at this issue in the same manner as long-term profit improvement projects.

Developing the Performance Measurement Blueprint. The blueprint measurement categories and priority weights direct the design of the scorecards. The scorecard design process should be a series of "cascading objectives" beginning with the organizational scorecard, moving to divisions, and then departments, teams, and individual employees. These "cascading objectives" ensure each lower organizational level is linked to the preceding level and, ultimately, to the organizational scorecard. Typically, as you move down through the organization, the measures shift from financial to non-financial with some exceptions like sales. The following table describes the typical measurement levels at each level of the organization.

Sample First Level Organizational Blueprint

DEPART.	SHORT-TERM PROFIT	LONG-TERM PROFIT PROJECTS	WORKING CAPITAL EFFICIENCY	CUSTOMER SERVICE	SAFETY
Sales	Gross Revenue GP Margin%	New Vendors Project Sales Training Project		Customer Satisfaction Survey	
Operations	Operating Ratio	Process Improved System Installed	Days Inventory Outstanding	%Ontime Delivery %Returns	OSHA Incident Rate
Accounting	On-time & Accurate Reporting % Budgets Met	Cost Acct. Installed New Pricing Completed	Days Sales Outstanding	Credit Approval Turnaround Time	

Organizational Level	Measurement Levels
Divisional Measures	Divisional budget outcomes and progress on the strategic plan
Departmental Measures	Departmental budget outcomes, progress on the strategic plan, team roll-ups
Team Measures	Team performance, departmental roll-downs, individual roll-ups.
Personal Measures	Personal performance, team roll-downs, peer ratings, attendance

Example of Organization with Team Level Scorecards

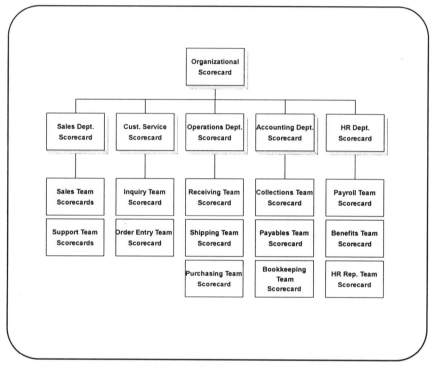

11.6 Characteristics of Good Performance Measures. The specific performance measures employed should be determined by five factors: alignment, validity, reliability, controllability, and data availability. An aligned measure is one that directly drives the results of the next organizational level outcome. The more closely the correlation between the measure and its "superior measure," the more aligned is the measure.

A valid measure accurately describes a performance result. Typically, valid measures must be objective, since subjective measures like ratings are often influenced by extraneous factors. The one exception is the customer satisfaction rating, since the customer's perception is the result.

Many results should be compared to work input to accurately describe performance. For example, number of errors is a valid result, but the performance measure would usually be more accurately presented as a ratio of errors to volume. A result of one error for two units produced describes a very different performance than one error for one thousand units produced.

A reliable measure is one that is consistent across time in its portrayal of performance. My first performance pay plan was for a bank's data entry operators. In my initial research I graphed performance across days, and discovered a consistent cycle in which more items were produced on Monday, less on Tuesday through Thursday, and again a high volume on Friday. Fresh out of academia, I excitedly believed I had discovered some universal behavioral law related to weekends.

I later found out that bank customers simply cash more checks and make more deposits on Monday and Friday. The cycle was due to opportunity — not to employee motivation. A reliable measure will adjust for cycles and other intrinsic work factors that are out of the control of employees (unless the cycle can be eliminated). This is usually accomplished by converting the measure to a ratio of work output to work input (opportunity). Such adjustments should not be made at the organizational level where staffing and product mix are determined.

Employee control means that the measure can be significantly and consistently affected by the employees to whom the measure is assigned. To assign measures to employees that they cannot influence because of a lack of authority, or a reliance on many other employees (measure defined at too high a level), is to create a "lottery" rather than a performance pay system.

On the other hand, each level of employees will want the measure to be 100 percent under their control. To accomplish this, the measure would have to be at the process level rather than the result level. Often, process measures are invalid and unreliable. For example, we could measure salespeople on how many customers they see, which is almost totally under their control. However, if they never sell anything to customers, the measure would be invalid at higher organizational levels.

Data availability is often a key determinant of what an organization chooses to measure in its performance pay plans. I once walked into a new client's office to find line printer printouts taped all over the walls. The manager and his assistant were busily reviewing the printouts. I asked them what they were doing. The reply was, "We thought we would find every measure we currently produce and divide it by every other measure to see if it might be useful as a performance pay measure!"

The blueprint priorities help the designer decide whether to use current data or create a new measure. If the priority weight is low, then a reasonably valid current measure will serve. But if the priority weight is high, I may need to design a new, more valid measure. Of course, the more in-place measures and data are employed in the performance pay system, the less tedious the measurement process will be and an explanation of the measure will be less needed.

References

[1] G.H. Felix and J.L. Riggs. *Productivity by the Objectives Matrix.* Corvallis, OR: Oregon Productivity Center, 1986.

[2] William B. Abernathy. *Designing and Managing an Organization-Wide Incentive Pay System.* Memphis, TN: Abernathy & Associates, 1990.

[3] William B. Abernathy, *How to Design Effective Incentive Plans.* Memphis, TN: Abernathy & Associates, 1993.

Chapter 12: Profit-Indexed Performance Pay

HOW A PROFIT-INDEXED PERFORMANCE PAY SYSTEM IS DESIGNED AND HOW THE SYSTEM IS LINKED TO THE PERFORMANCE SCORECARDS.

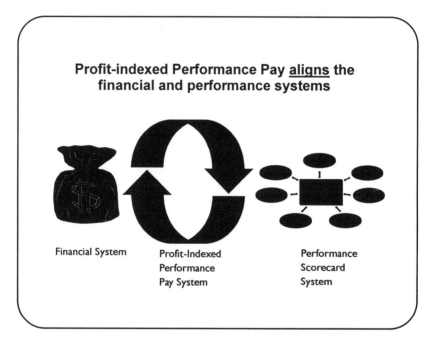

Profit-indexed Performance Pay <u>aligns</u> the financial and performance systems

Financial System   Profit-Indexed Performance Pay System   Performance Scorecard System

System Architecture. Profit-Indexed Performance Pay (PIPP) links the performance scorecards to the financial success of the organization through a performance pay system. The goal of PIPP is to provide an organization-wide pay system that is an alternative to the conventional wage-and-salary system.

The monthly employee performance pay opportunity is generally computed from a three-month rolling average of organizational or, alternatively, divisional net income gains. This opportunity is then distributed to employees based upon

141

their performance scores. These scores are computed through the Performance Scorecard.

In the advanced phase of PIPP, employees forego annual wage and salary increases in exchange for increases in performance pay opportunity. Employees share some of the organization's risks in exchange for a greater share of the company's success — termed "profit-indexed pay." Profit-indexed pay makes partners of employees whose pay is no longer tied to entitlements or internal politics, but rather to the success of the organization and personal contribution to that success.

There are three key components to PIPP. These are the employee *performance pay basis*, the *organizational multiplier*, and the *Performance Scorecard*.

The Performance Pay Basis. Each employee is assigned a performance pay basis. The basis is expressed as a percentage of the employee's wage or salary. For example, an employee with a monthly salary of $2,000, and a basis of five percent would have a $2,000 X 5% = $100 monthly base performance pay opportunity. The basis percentage can vary among employees to adjust for organizational level, increased competencies, years of service, or changes in the market value of a job.

The basis may be increased each year in lieu of annual wage-and-salary increases. The employee is given a greater share of the organization's success in exchange for less guaranteed pay. Typically, this exchange is a three-to-one ratio to compensate for the fact that performance pay is not guaranteed. A multiplier that ranged to three would provide this ratio so the basis increase is the same as the foregone salary increase.

142

The Organizational Multiplier. The organizational multiplier typically ranges from zero to three in the initial phase of PIPP. Over time, the upper limit may be increased. The multiplier value is determined by gains in organizational or divisional net income. In many cases, selected revenues and expenses may be removed from the calculation of net income. These revenues and expenses are considered largely uncontrollable by the majority of employees. This adjusted net income is termed "Controllable Net Income" (CNI). The Controllable Net Income is usually computed as the rolling average of the current and past two months.

The CNI value at which the multiplier is zero is termed the "threshold." This value includes a predefined return on investment to ownership (or reserve for non-profits), as well as the average monthly net result of revenues and expenses excluded from the computation of the CNI. Multiplier values above zero are computed from a "share percentage" selected in advance. The multiplier scale is reviewed and adjusted each year based upon changes in return-on-investment requirements, uncontrollable revenues and expenses, and the payroll. The following are examples of how CNI is defined, followed by an organization-wide multiplier scale.

P&L Line	?	Controllable	?	Non-Controllable
Gross Sales	X	$2,000,000		0
Capital Sales			X	N/A
Payroll	X	$400,000		0
Benefits	X	$30,000		0
Occupancy			X	$20,000
Repairs, Mtnce	X	$40,000		0
Materials Expense	X	$600,000		0
Inventory Expense	X	$130,000		0
L-T Debt Service			X	$80,000
Marktg & Advert			X	$60,000
Utilities	X	$15,000		0
Wkmns Comp	X	$20,000		0
Depreciation			X	$105,000
NET		$1,235,000		($265,000)

Minimum Acceptable Profit: $500,000

+ Avg Uncontrollable Expenses: $265,000

= Multiplier Threshold: $765,000

Sample Multiplier Scale

allows to compute compare apples to apples

CONTROLLABLE NET INCOME	MULTIPLIER
765,000	0.00
845,000	1.00
865,000	1.25
885,000	1.50
905,000	1.75
925,000	2.00
945,000	2.25
965,000	2.50
985,000	2.75
1,050,000	3.00

→ **When the multiplier is at 2.00, the performance pay opportunity is 5% X 2 = 10%**
(Basis x Multiplier = Opportunity)

12.5 Each employee's personal basis percentage is adjusted by the organizational multiplier to compute the month's performance pay opportunity. This opportunity is expressed as a percentage of the employee's wage or salary.

For example, if the organization's three-month rolling average CNI was $925,000 on the above example scale, then the multiplier for the month would be 2.0. An employee with a five percent basis would then have a 2.0 x 5% = 10% of salary performance pay opportunity. An employee with a ten percent basis would have a 2.0 x 10% = 20% of salary opportunity.

The Performance Scorecard. The Performance Scorecard was described in the previous chapter. To compute an employee's performance pay, the performance pay opportunity (basis x multiplier) is multiplied by the performance index of the scorecard to which the employee is assigned. In a divisional PIPP, all employees in the same division would be assigned the same performance index. In a departmental plan, all employees in the same department would be assigned the same performance index. In a team plan, all team members would be assigned the same performance index, while in a personal plan each employee's index would be determined by his personal scorecard. In many cases, a blend of levels would make up an employee's scorecard. The following table lists various combinations of these computations.

	Employee Salary	Incent. Basis	Incent. Multiplier	Perf. Index	Payout
A)	$2,000	5%	0.00	100%	$ 0
B)	$2,000	5%	1.50	100%	$150
C)	$2,000	5%	3.00	100%	$300
D)	$2,000	5%	3.00	50%	$150
E)	$2,000	5%	3.00	00%	$ 0
F)	$2,000	10%	3.00	100%	$600

Handwritten annotations: 12.6 ; 0% - 100% ; How well you performed ; =2050 ; Employee decides ; Org decides ; Employee determines

In example (A) the employee receives no performance payout because the organizational performance pay multiplier has not exceeded the minimum threshold.

In (B) Controllable Net Income was sufficient to produce a 1.5 multiplier which created a 7.5 percent performance pay opportunity for the employee (5% x 1.5). The employee received 7.5 percent, or $150, because the Performance Scorecard's index was at 100 percent.

In (C) the employee received the maximum payout percentage, given the 5 percent basis (3 x 5% = 15%) for a $300 payout.

In (D) the maximum performance pay opportunity was available but the employee only received 50 percent of it because the assigned scorecard was at 50 percent (5% x 3 x 50% = 7.5% x $2,000 = $150).

In (E) the maximum performance pay opportunity is again available, but because the assigned scorecard is at 0 percent, no payout is made.

Finally, in (F) the employee has been assigned a greater personal performance pay basis of 10 percent which creates a 30 percent maximum opportunity and a $600 payout due to a PI of 100 percent. The key features of PIPP are:

1) *Payout linked to organizational net income.* Performance pay is directly linked to organizational net income. No performance pay payout will occur if the organization fails to generate a minimum return on investment and cover its uncontrollable expenses. As a result, performance pay is always "affordable" for the organization. Further, employees become partners in the long-term success of the overall

organization or division. The result is a personal interest in cooperatively improving revenues and controlling expenses.

2) Payout linked to key performances. Performance pay is also directly linked to departmental, small team and/or individual objective performance measures. Those who contribute more to the success of the organization earn more. Further, these measures establish performance goals for employees on results they directly affect. The scorecards precisely describe each employee's role in the organization's mission and provide monthly feedback regarding performance compared to base and goal.

3) Payout linked to personal market value and risk. Performance pay opportunity is also determined by each employee's personal performance pay basis percentage. Employees whose skills and experience have a high market value are assigned a higher basis. Employees who share business risks with the organization through below market wages and salaries are also assigned higher performance pay bases to reward this risktaking.

Chapter 13: Positive Leadership

POSITIVE LEADERSHIP AND THE LEADERSHIP GRID ARE EXPLAINED. THE BENEFITS OF POSITIVE LEADERSHIP TO THE ORGANIZATION AND INDIVIDUAL MANAGERS ARE DESCRIBED.

When I began my career in designing performance pay systems, I believed that the introduction of objective performance measurement and performance pay would significantly reduce the management role and even eliminate it in some cases. I assumed that once workers were directly able to affect their pay, they would become overnight entrepreneurs who would not require management intervention. This proved, over a period of years, to be a naive viewpoint.

The reasons new businesses fail are underfunding, poor business plans, a lack of management ability, and an unwillingness to continue to assume the risks associated with self-employment. The same issues arise within an organization. Employees who enter a shared risk-reward pay system find they can't earn enough to remain in the system. They can't understand their business plan (scorecard), lack the skills to meet the goals, and are unwilling to assume the risks. It is the manager's role to help employees make this *13.)* difficult transition. Unlike a self-employed individual, the employee entrepreneur has the resources of a functioning organization and the direct support of a professional manager.

It is the manager who must support the employee in making the transition from directed subordinate to empowered, self-managed entrepreneur. Performance pay and objective goals alone will foster this change in only a limited number of cases. My term for the management philosophy and techniques that enable this transition is *Positive Leadership*.

The philosophy of Positive Leadership is to delegate authority and accountability wherever possible, and to design jobs and structure workflow to facilitate independent employee action. Positive leaders see themselves more as customers than as managers. That is, they determine what the organization needs from each employee and purchase these products and services from the employee who becomes more a vendor than a subordinate.

Further, the positive leader wants these services at a good price, high quality, on time, and to specification. These expectations are defined by the leader in the Performance Scorecard. The leader must serve as the "bridge" between the organization's external customers and its employees.

To move employees from order-takers and entitlement thinkers requires a unique set of skills from the positive leader. The leader must change from management by perception and exception to management of incremental improvements in objective results. Further, the leader must change from a command role to a support role. A successful positive leader is one who ensures that employees know what the organization wants and provides the tools and resources to meet these needs.

The specific skill set of the positive leader includes:

√ Performance Analysis

√ Performance Improvement

√ Performance Coaching

Performance Analysis. Many manager and supervisor training programs don't include the analysis of employee performance in the curriculum. These analyses are not common knowledge and must be learned. Broadly, there are three types of performance analyses that are useful to managers and supervisors; trend analysis, variance analysis, and process analysis.

Trend Analysis. Most of us look at performance as a "snapshot." But performance occurs through time. To accurately analyze performance, the trend or change in performance over time must be examined. The goal is continuous incremental improvement (positive trend). What should be recognized is steady, positive trends, not just one-time exceptional performances. Flat or negative trends should signal the need for a performance improvement plan, rather than one-time instances of poor performance.

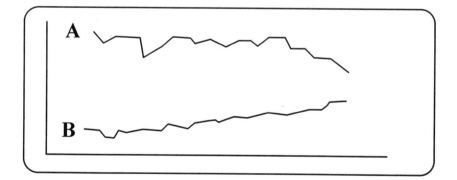

In the above example, who needs assistance, employee A or B? If we looked only at the *most recent* performance, we would spend our time working with B rather than A because B's current performance is lower than A's.

Variance Analysis. Variance analysis refers to the variability in performance from period to period rather than the overall trend. Two types of variance analysis are especially useful in performance analysis. These are variance across time and variance among employees.

Performance variance across time has been analyzed extensively using the method of *Statistical Process Control* (SPC). Increases in variance across time indicate problems in processes, materials, or opportunity to perform.

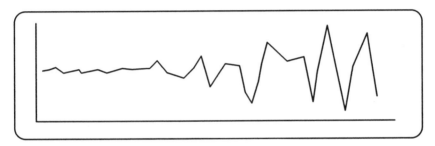

Performance variances among employees indicate skills, training, work distribution, or work process differences.

Process Analysis. Process analysis refers to the analysis of the processes underlying the results measures found on the Performance Scorecard. This analysis usually follows an opportunity identified by trend or variance analysis. Two examples of first-level process analyses are provided for sales and productivity performances. Once the first-level problem is identified, a second-level analysis must be performed to correct the problem.

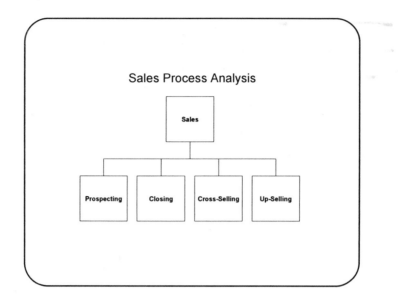

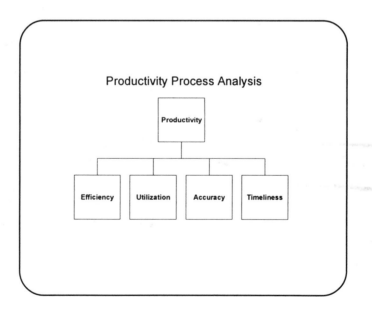

153

Performance Improvement. Performance improvement plans should be developed only after a performance analysis has been conducted to pinpoint performances with the most improvement opportunity. Examples of performance improvement plans include process improvements, work scheduling, cross-training, work distribution, ergonomics, job aids, automation, and others. Whatever plan is implemented, the effect on the performance measure should be monitored to determine the success of the plan.

Performance Coaching. It is a difficult task for the conventional manager to move away from negative management to positive management. Years of experience in direct supervision in a conventional entitlement pay system must be overcome. But the rewards are great. Positive managers find they are allies of employees rather than adversaries. They find themselves spending much less time in direct supervision and firefighting, and more time planning and improving work processes. They find their area more predictable and their employees more dependable.

Leadership Grid. The two dimensions of positive management are defining and obtaining results, and the implementation of Positive Leadership techniques. These two dimensions are portrayed on the following Leadership Grid.

154

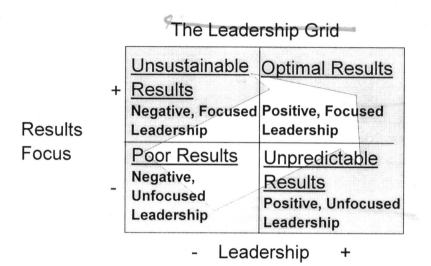

The Leadership Grid

	Unsustainable Results	Optimal Results
+	Negative, Focused Leadership	Positive, Focused Leadership
-	Poor Results	Unpredictable Results
	Negative, Unfocused Leadership	Positive, Unfocused Leadership

Results Focus

-    Leadership   +

The Leadership Grid describes the two aspects of Positive Leadership: a focus on improvement in objective results, and a transition from negative to Positive Leadership practices. There are four quadrants, each describing a different leadership approach.

The lower left quadrant (poor results) describes a manager who relies on perceptions and exceptions to manage subordinates and fails to objectively specify desired outcomes and goals for them. This style of management produces the poorest results.

The upper left (unsustainable results) quadrant describes a manager who precisely states what the desired outcomes and goals are, but relies on intimidation and subjective impressions to manage people toward achieving these results. This approach to management produces results in the short-term, but it is difficult to consistently sustain the results.

The lower right quadrant (unpredictable results) depicts a manager who is supportive and doesn't employ intimidation to manage. However, the manager fails to specify desired outcomes, leaving subordinates the task of translating organizational objectives into job-level goals. The results are unpredictable since the manager's subordinates are often not in a position to make an effective translation.

The upper right quadrant (optimal results) describes a manager who is both results-focused and uses positive management to achieve these results. This style will produce optimal results that are sustainable over the long term.

Leadership Feedback. A manager's leadership can be assessed by comparing the performance of his area to a subordinate survey of the manager's effectiveness in the practice of Positive Leadership behaviors. This relationship between area performance and leadership can be plotted quarterly on a grid as illustrated on the following page.

THE LEADERSHIP GRID

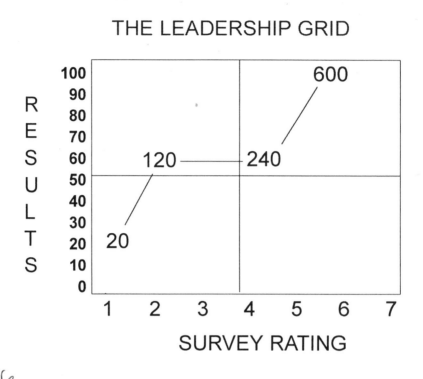

1 3 . 6 **Problems with managing through negative reinforcement.**
Though fear is an effective motivator, it carries with it several adverse side effects that make it a less effective, long-term management strategy than positive reinforcement. These side effects include:

1. Absenteeism and tardiness as employees avoid the highly unpleasant, fear-driven workplace.

2. Increased turnover proportionate to the use of fear as a management tool.

3. Anxiety produced by threats and criticism which is usually counterproductive, especially in highly skilled jobs or jobs requiring direct customer contact.

4. The need for a high level of expensive, direct supervision to use fear effectively.

5. The perception that the supervisor is an adversary. As a result, she is much less effective in coaching and assisting employees to improve performance. Employees who lack skills will hide their deficiencies rather than ask for help to correct them.

6. A reduction in employee initiative and creativity. Constructive suggestions for improving processes may be withheld.

7. Retaliation from employees who strike back through constant complaining, work slowdowns, sabotage, and theft.

8. Peer pressure directed toward minimum performance when increased management expectations lead to higher standards and more threats and reprisals.

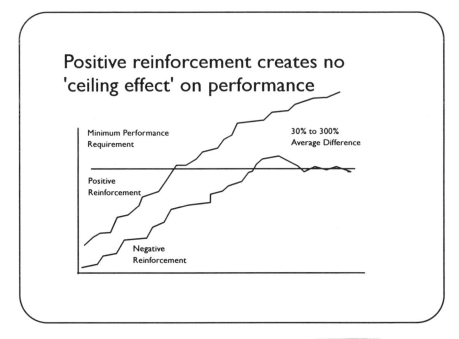

Positive reinforcement creates no 'ceiling effect' on performance

Minimum Performance Requirement

30% to 300% Average Difference

Positive Reinforcement

Negative Reinforcement

Advantages to managing through positive reinforcement.

1. Employees will seek to continuously improve rather than simply performing at the minimum standard.

2. Morale will increase while absenteeism and turnover decrease.

3. Less direct supervision is required. Fewer supervisors are needed. Supervisors can spend more time forecasting, scheduling, coaching and improving processes.

4. An untapped resource will emerge. Given concrete objectives, feedback, and incentives, employees will show more initiative and creativity in improving processes and working with their peers.

An organization that relies on positive reinforcement isn't "managed" in the traditional sense. Employees understand the organization's goals and how they contribute to them. Employees personally share in organizational success, and work with each other on a more equal plane. The manager-worker adversarial relationship is replaced with a true sense of common purpose and partnership.

Chapter 14: Toward an Entrepreneurial Workplace

A DESIGN AND IMPLEMENTATION STRATEGY FOR A *TOTAL PERFORMANCE SYSTEM* IS DISCUSSED. THE CHARACTERISTICS OF A PROACTIVE EMPLOYEE GROUP AND ENTREPRENEURIAL WORKPLACE ARE DESCRIBED AND A TRANSITION STRATEGY IS EXPLAINED.

Total Performance System Design and Implementation Strategy. The following strategy has proven efficient and effective in the design and implementation of TPS. The steps listed are detailed in Chapters 10 through 13.

I. Performance Scorecard Design

    A. Design Organizational Scorecard

    B. Develop Performance Measurement Blueprint

    C. Define Division Level Scorecards

    D. Define Department Level Scorecards

    E. Define Team Scorecards

    F. Define Personal Scorecards

II. Profit-Indexed Performance Pay Design

    A. Define Multiplier Calculation Level

    B. Define Controllable Net Income

    C. Define Employee Performance Pay Basis Percent

    D. Define Multiplier Scale Threshold

    E. Define Performance Pay Share Percentage

F. Compute Multiplier Scale

G. Test Performance Pay Opportunity With Historical Data And Revise If Necessary

III. *Develop TPS Administration*

A. Develop Data Capture Methods

B. Install System Database And Conduct Trial Run

C. Prepare System Documentation

D. Prepare Employee Orientations And Materials

E. Train Performance System Managers

IV. *TPS Rollout and Employee Orientations*

A. Prepare First Scorecards And Performance Payroll

B. Verify and Edit Scorecards And Payroll

C. Conduct Positive Leadership Training

D. Conduct Employee Orientations

V. *TPS Refinement Phase*

A. Validate Monthly Results For Six-Month Period

B. Revise System Monthly To Improve Validity

C. Pinpoint Performance Improvement Opportunities

D. Implement Performance Improvement Plans

VI. Transition to Variable Pay

    A. Audit Total Performance System Validity

    B. Conduct Wage and Salary Survey

    C. Prepare Employee Orientations and Materials

    D. Conduct *Open Book Management* Sessions

    E. Implement Base Pay Freeze and Performance Pay Basis Increase

    F. Provide Volunteer Base Pay Reduction Option

    G. Reinstitute Base Pay Increases When Below Market Goal Met

The Proactive Employee. Each year thousands of people start their own businesses. Statistics show that some seventy percent of these businesses fail within three years. If the transition from worker to entrepreneur is so difficult, why should employees even try? The advantages to the organization have been stated — but what's in it for the individual employee?

In B.F. Skinner's book *Contingencies of Reinforcement: A Theoretical Analysis* [1], he explained that humans are genetically built to "operate" on their environments. Many other species survive through instinctive behavior patterns that are present at birth. Birds don't learn to peck or make nests — these activities are instinctive. Humans, on the other hand, come into the world with few instincts and must learn to survive. Unlike most other animals, human infants are unable to survive on their own for many years.

Because humans learn to operate on their environments, they are much more adaptable than most other species. Few species prosper in as many diverse ecological niches as do humans. You find humans surviving in the polar region and the jungles, in the deserts and in the marshes, and even in space. This is possible because each person is constantly testing the environment and adjusting to changes.

It is the need for environmental control — for a connection between what we do and results — that defines us. As mentioned previously, Skinner points out that the word satiated (full) is derived from the Greek work "sated" or sad. Common wisdom generally supports Skinner's theory. When I was in graduate school, the students talked about post-doctoral depression. Many students find that once they receive their degree they experience an emptiness, rather than the elation they anticipated. The same experience often holds true for people who retire.

In talking with hundreds of people in all sorts of companies, I find many employees who tried self-employment at one point in their careers but returned to the employee role. When we discuss the two situations, I have never had a person tell me they would not return to self-employment if they could figure out how to make it work for them. The opportunity to directly control outcomes — to do what you think needs to be done, rather than what you're told to do — essentially defines the American dream.

Global competition has caused the American manager to take a hard look at our management practices. Curiously, many have chosen to look outward for a solution, particularly to Japan, rather than inward to what made us so successful in the first place. This outward search is especially odd when you consider the reaffirmation of our free enterprise system after the collapse of communism across the world.

As George Gilder has stated, economists and management theorists have tended to focus on large corporations to analyze American business, when the true core of our innovation and success has been our entrepreneurial, small businesses. We should look to companies in their formative stages for solutions to performance problems. It is our entrepreneurial class that will ensure our competitiveness in the future.

The one word that best summarizes the characteristics of the American entrepreneurial class is "proactive." In seminars with business leaders, I have asked them what they thought being proactive meant. The following is a list of characteristics that they are looking for in a proactive employee.

1. Initiators. Proactive employees don't have to be told what to do: they are self-starters. Proactive employees don't require or want continuous, direct supervision.

2. Decision-Makers. Proactive employees make decisions on their own. They are creative and don't depend on management to make every decision.

3. Consistent. Proactive employees aren't a flash in the pan. They perform well under adversity and over the long haul.

4. Self-Employed. Proactive employees think and act like they are self-employed. They don't need constant reassurances from others to get the job done.

5. Team Players. Successful proactive employees aren't loners. They know that to get the job done they must work with the team.

165

6. Aligned. Proactive employees understand the big picture. They see their personal success as linked to the company's success.

1. & 2. Initiators and Decision-Makers. Proactive employees don't have to be told what to do. They think creatively on their own.

Once a performance pay plan is designed, an orientation meeting is held for the participating employees. In one such meeting, I was explaining how a reduction in the throughput time of checks in a bank's item processing area would save the bank money. These savings would be shared with the employees. The group listened intently. The savings associated with throughput had never been explained to them, even though some had been in the job several years. The employees entered into a lively discussion and in one meeting rerouted the entire courier system, which significantly reduced the bank's throughput time.

In a similar meeting, the productivity of a medical lab's word processing group was hampered by the erratic nature of job requests. There were days when there was nothing to do. The group met and developed a plan to contract out their word processing to client hospitals. Word processing became a profit center for the lab.

If you gave your employees a test on how your business makes a profit, how many would pass? Most companies fail to share their business plan with the people who make it happen — their employees. They don't take the time to show employees how their specific job role affects the overall plan. Instead they offer their employees vague slogans like "quality is everything." No one can be proactive, and we wouldn't

166

want them to be, without some idea of what their organization is trying to accomplish.

Your employees are as smart as you let them be.

3. Consistent. Proactive employees are steady, reliable high performers.

An assertion made by some management theorists is that when the work process is refined, employees automatically perform at their peak ability. They tell us that ineffective procedures are the only obstacle to consistent, high levels of employee performance.

To me, this assertion is wishful thinking. It defies common sense and our personal experiences. How effectively each of us works at a task is determined by our motivation to complete the task, as much as it is by how we go about accomplishing the task. Few people are effective at a job they don't want to do. To foster a proactive employee group, we need to pay as much attention to motivation as we do to techniques.

Don't tell me how until you tell me why.

A universal obstacle to consistent high performance is the conventional pay system. When you pay employees by the hour, you encourage "pacing." Employees slow down to ensure a full day's pay and to receive overtime pay. Supervisors come to manage time rather than results. Employees who finish early are criticized for having nothing to do.

Busyness isn't Business. When you pay for time, you get time. When you pay for results, you get results.

4. Self-employed. Proactive employees think and act like they are self-employed. Proactive employees don't require constant reassurances from others to be persistent and effective at their jobs.

Psychologist B.F. Skinner pointed out how we admire the person who persists at a seemingly unpleasant task without external pressure or guidance from others. For example, the writer or researcher who works long hours with no external supervision, or the worker who day after day arrives at work on time and performs consistently and independently. Because we see no external controls, we assume the person must have been born this way.

However, the unsupervised worker is really not such a mystery. He has simply learned to relate directly to the long-term results of his efforts and no longer needs a supervisor as an intermediary. The typist on a salary may produce documents to avoid supervisor criticism. In contrast, the self-employed typist works to satisfy his customers. Similarly, self-employed accountants, attorneys, programmers, salespeople, and so on, have learned to work for customers rather than supervisors.

Learning to be self-employed is learning to work *for* results instead of working to *avoid* criticism. The successful self-employed individual learns to work for often unpredictable, long-delayed pay and recognition without the need of day-to-day supervision. A proactive workplace provides employees the opportunity to learn to perform like self-employed people. Performance is linked directly to work outcomes. Earnings opportunities increase but also are somewhat less predictable. Creating a proactive employee group means gradually introducing risk into the pay system in exchange for more personal freedom and opportunity.

Risk is: The price you have to pay to be free.

5. Team Players. Successful proactive employees aren't loners. They know that to get the job done they must work with the team.

In the past decade many management theorists have emphasized the work team over the individual employee. Though cooperation is certainly important, it should be remembered that if none of the individual employees on a team do any work, the team doesn't get any work done!

People are not naturally uncooperative. If employees aren't cooperating, we should ask why. Three traditional management practices discourage cooperation; competitive recognition programs, competitive compensation and promotion practices, and failure to reinforce team contributions.

6. Aligned: Creating a Proactive Workplace. Proactive employees understand the big picture. They see their personal success as linked to the company's success.

Most managers admire these individuals' entrepreneurial spirits and wish their own employee group would be more proactive rather than reactive "order-takers." But they have constructed a work environment that is autocratic and paternalistic. When the banking industry was deregulated and banks had to compete for accounts, many banks made sales a new priority. These banks conducted sales training programs but were often disappointed with the results. In desperation, they fired their lenders and branch managers and replaced them with "real" salespeople like stock brokers.

However, with the change in personnel there was no concurrent change in the banks' performance systems. The pay system remained conventional. The duties were simply expanded to include sales rather than redesigned to provide time for sales. The bureaucracy remained intact; there was no change in management style. The result was that many stock brokers soon began to act like conventional bankers. Moreover, many of the displaced bankers proved to be successful salespeople in the stock broker environment.

The lesson is, if you want employees aligned with organizational goals, you must create an environment that supports these goals.

A Phased Transition Strategy Toward an Entrepreneurial Workplace. An entrepreneurial workplace asks employees to share the organization's financial risks and rewards through a variable pay system. Further, employees are asked to move from reactive to proactive job roles and to assume an accountability for results instead of effort. This is a difficult transition for people, as witnessed by the high failure rate of people who try to start their own businesses.

I personally experienced the trauma of self-reliance when I resigned a position as a tenured college professor to move to self-employment. I remember sitting in my apartment day after day waiting for a check that never came. It finally occurred to me it wasn't going to come until I left the apartment and found a client.

The best strategy for moving an employee group from an entitlement culture toward an entrepreneurial one is to make the transition gradually, to phase in the change. Two organizational changes have to occur simultaneously for the most effective transition. First, the management style must move from traditional management by perception and exception toward Positive Leadership. Instead of recognizing employees they like, managers must recognize those who perform well on objective criteria. Instead of waiting for mistakes and then punishing employees for them, managers must continuously measure performance and recognize and manage improvements.

This management change has proven to be difficult in practice. Managers and supervisors with years of experience in managing "entitled" employees without performance data have developed a management style that is difficult to overcome. We all prefer to recognize those we like. We all prefer to exert the least effort possible. It is more effort to continually measure performance than to simply react to exceptions. However, if managers fail to make the transition, it will be impossible for the organization to move toward an entrepreneurial workplace.

Once Positive Leadership is installed, the second necessary prerequisite for a successful transition is that the pay system move from one of entitlement toward one of shared risk and reward. The key ingredient in entrepreneurial behavior is moderate risk coupled with high opportunity. This conclusion was arrived at by the psychologist David McClelland who analyzed entrepreneurs over many years and cultures [1].

In one of his more famous studies, he asked subjects to toss rings at a post. The subject could stand wherever he wished. Some subjects stood directly over the post and dropped the rings on the post. Others stood far away while another group chose to stand a moderate distance where success was possible but not a given. When McClelland compared the three groups to independent measures of entrepreneurship, he found that those who stood over the post or far away were not entrepreneurial. Those who chose a moderate risk of failure were found to be the most entrepreneurial.

In the workplace, moderate risk coupled with high opportunity would translate to pay somewhat below the local market with incentive earnings well above market. Currently, I find the optimal arrangement to be that wages and salaries range 15 percent to 30 percent below market with a performance pay opportunity of 30 percent to 60 percent above market. This arrangement can be achieved over a period of time by simply freezing annual wage-and-salary increases while annually increasing employee performance pay opportunity (bases). The effect of a wage-and-salary freeze on a given employee would depend upon his performance. High performers would, assuming the company was profitable, do much better than market. Average performers would remain at market, while poor performers would fall below market.

An organization can accelerate the transition by reducing wages and salaries rather than simply freezing annual increases. I recommend that this approach be applied cautiously, and that it be implemented as a voluntary program. The final table in this section describes a two-phased approach to the transition from entitlement pay and negative management to shared risk-reward and Positive Leadership.

Though many management and leadership programs attempt to shift managers away from negative management, they fail to emphasize or create the two conditions necessary for the shift — performance measurement and shared risk. As long as these factors are missing from an organization, it cannot move toward Positive Leadership.

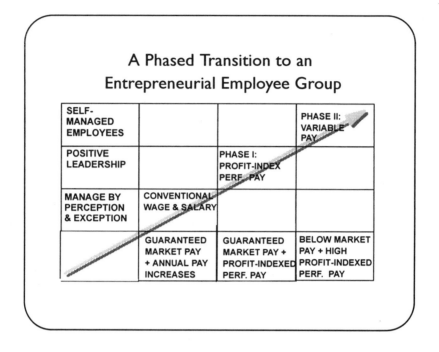

A Phased Transition to an Entrepreneurial Employee Group

SELF-MANAGED EMPLOYEES			PHASE II: VARIABLE PAY
POSITIVE LEADERSHIP		PHASE I: PROFIT-INDEX PERF. PAY	
MANAGE BY PERCEPTION & EXCEPTION	CONVENTIONAL WAGE & SALARY		
	GUARANTEED MARKET PAY + ANNUAL PAY INCREASES	GUARANTEED MARKET PAY + PROFIT-INDEXED PERF. PAY	BELOW MARKET PAY + HIGH PROFIT-INDEXED PERF. PAY

Creating a Risk-Taking Employee Group. Fifty years of entitlement pay and management by exception make it difficult to move an employee group from risk-averse, entitlement thinking to shared risk takers. To succeed, the organization must remove as many obstacles to entrepreneurial risk-taking as possible. The following is a list of seven of the most common risk-taking factors an organization must attempt to overcome as it moves toward an entrepreneurial, shared risk-reward pay workplace.

Risk-Taking Factors. There are two classes of risks the employee faces when moving from entitlement pay and subjective management to shared risk-reward and objective management. The first risk is personal — the employee must accept responsibility and accountability for accomplishing

173

the desired job outcomes. The second risk is interpersonal — the employee must have faith and trust in his peers, and in the organization that it will be supportive and successful.

Personal Risks

1. Skills — Do I know how to meet the goals?

2. Effort — Do I want to invest the effort to meet the goals?

3. Change — Have I been so successful in the conventional system that the risk of moving to a new system is too great?

Interpersonal Risks

4. Faith — Do I believe my organization will be successful?

5. Trust — Will management fairly share with me if I perform well?

6. Opportunity — Will the organizational structure and resources be in place to enable me to consistently meet the goals?

7. Help — Will management and my peers support my efforts?

1. Skills — Do I know how to meet the goals? Employees will be reluctant to take on more accountability, or link their pay to performance, if they feel they don't have the skills needed to maximize their performance and performance pay payouts. A lack of training might prevent employees from meeting the goals. This obstacle should be corrected prior to moving toward any significant risk or opportunity situation. Training should include specific job skills, but also a knowledge of how the organization operates and training in process improvement methods.

2. Effort — Do I want to invest the effort to meet the goals?
Employees who have operated in an entitlement environment
managed through exception may believe that the effort required to become entrepreneurial, and ensure a good living,
is too great. Years of disconnect between effort and reward
create this attitude of "learned helplessness," as described by
the psychologist Martin Seligman. The solution is to implement the system in graduated phases. Each phase should be
designed to minimize failure and maximize success.

The key to overcoming this attitude is to enable employees to
"win" early in the introduction of performance pay. Many
companies pride themselves on designing performance pay
systems that don't pay out. My response is, why have a performance pay system at all? The organization must define a
plan that pays out something for small, incremental improvements over current performance.

The employees must be able to immediately and consistently
see results for their efforts. This will reestablish the natural
connection between work and rewards lost by the entitlement
system. This "learned effectiveness" can be further hastened
by frequent social recognition during the early stages of the
system's implementation.

Finally, managers and supervisors must be trained in advance
in Positive Leadership strategies that replace management by
perception and exception. If the old practices carry forward
into the new performance pay system, they will retard or prevent the development of entrepreneurial employees.

*3. Change — Have I been so successful in the conventional
system that the risk of moving to a new system is too great?* I
am often asked, "Which employees will most resist the

175

introduction of performance pay?" The answer may be a surprise. I find line supervisors most resistant followed closely by middle managers. Next I find top workers resistant and average workers least resistant.

Why is this? The level of resistance is directly proportional to the employee's personal investment, success, and opportunity within the entitlement pay system. The supervisor and middle manager have to change more than anyone else to *Hang* move to an entrepreneurial workplace. They must move from autocratic management by perception and exception to employee empowerment and the positive management of results.

The top worker has been successful in the entitlement workplace and can't be sure how he will fare in a performance-based system. If an employee is well liked, has seniority, is next in line for a promotion, and has the right job experience and education, he has the most to lose from any change in the pay and management system. — *9 Also commetary*

It is the average employee who has the most to gain from performance-based pay. The employee with limited education and job experience is not marketable in a "commodity" oriented pay system. The employee who is not politically adroit is doomed to low pay and little advancement in the organization. For these employees, performance-based pay is the only way out — it is the only way they will share in the American dream. *meeting can help w/ info*

The employee who was successful in the entitlement system often learned to negotiate his success. Everything becomes negotiable: work assignments, deadlines, performance goals attendance and more. In the entrepreneurial workplace, objective performance goals are established and must be considered *nonnegotiable* once they are established.

Perhaps, the most serious error management can make in the transition to an entrepreneurial workplace is to allow the entitlement practice of negotiation to continue. Negotiation in a performance-based system occurs in the goal-setting process and in after-the-fact adjustments to performance results. Negotiation maintains the subjective, political characteristics of the entitlement system. Personal success in the organization remains how well you negotiate with your superior, rather than what you accomplish.

A self-employed person cannot negotiate success. Profits are what they are and a lack of profitability cannot be changed through excuses and explanations. A farmer can't negotiate away bad weather nor a retailer unsatisfied customers. Real life isn't always fair. Sometimes we try and fail because of circumstances outside our control.

4. Faith — Do I believe my organization will be successful?
An employee shares in the financial risks of the organization by exchanging guaranteed pay for a share of the organization's success. This is very much like investing in the company. When purchasing stock in a company, a wise investor reviews the financial history and business plan of the company before investing. Similarly, the organization must share its financials and business plan with its employees for them to invest their guaranteed pay in the company's performance.

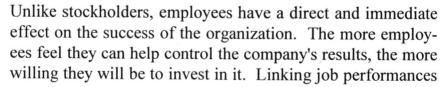

Unlike stockholders, employees have a direct and immediate effect on the success of the organization. The more employees feel they can help control the company's results, the more willing they will be to invest in it. Linking job performances to organizational results is a step in this direction. Management must explain these links and their effects on overall profitability and the achievement of the business plan. "Open Book Management" is a prerequisite to a successful transition to an entrepreneurial workplace.

5. Trust — Will management fairly share with me if I perform well? The greatest setback toward the transition to an entrepreneurial workplace is when management promises to award performance payouts for certain levels of organizational and personal performance, and then reneges on its promise. This failure not only affects current employees, but also employees for the life of the company since the story is handed down to new employees.

Management typically reneges on its promises in one of two ways. First, a plan is designed in which it is impossible for employees to earn incentives. The simple answer is don't install a plan unless you intend to pay out at least modest incentives.

Second, payouts occur but are rapidly followed by increases in profit and/or performance requirements. Most of us are familiar with what happened to the "piece-rate" pay system in manufacturing in the 1920s and '30s. Greedy owners continuously increased the piece-rate requirement until employees could not earn a reasonable living. If you expect employees to take on the financial risks with you, you must be willing to pay well above market wages and salaries when the company does well.

In my travels, over and over I am told the same sad story of a start-up company in which key salespeople were paid lucrative commissions. Once the company became stable, ownership cut back the commission rate. In many cases, the salesperson went to work for a competitor or became a competitor. Short-term greed will destroy any attempt to create an entrepreneurial employee group. The simple solution is that whenever employees' performance requirements are increased, their performance pay opportunity should be increased proportionately. That is, if you want more, offer more.

6. Opportunity — Will management and my peers support my efforts? Employees may know how to meet the goal, and may trust management to implement reasonable goals, but may feel there are other organizational constraints that will prevent consistent goal attainment. Three common constraints include inconsistent work volumes, inefficient work processes, and excessive off-task assignments.

Inconsistent work volumes will affect most performance goals in production areas. There simply may not be enough work to do in a given cycle or season. Two solutions are cross-training and flexible scheduling. With cross-training an employee moves out of a low-volume area to a high-volume area and thus reduces the decrease in pay. Flexible scheduling offers employees time off in exchange for leaving the organization during potential low opportunity periods.

In addition to time off, some organizations assign performance credit to employees who, during low-volume cycles, succeed at training or participate in value-added projects that are critical to the organization's strategic plan. A special credit performance measure can be added to the scorecard to provide for these situations. However, special credit should only be assigned for work performed outside the employee's department.

179

Inefficient work processes can be overcome by chartering and training employee process improvement teams. If management implements team ideas, employees will gain a sense of control over their performance and earnings.

Excessive off-task assignments are a problem particularly for smaller organizations where it is difficult to design stable job positions. However, larger organizations may also experience this problem when job assignments have not been clearly specified, or when staffing is not done with proper forethought. An obstacle for any organization is that in the conventional system, moving people around is relatively easy since only exceptions are measured and pay is linked to time rather than performance. Managers will have difficulty adjusting to the more rigorous requirements of performance-based pay in this regard.

This problem can be largely handled in the design of the system. If performance results are specified at "higher" organizational levels, rather than at a process or job level, movement across functions will still reward employees in the area. Second, "loaned and borrowed" team hours reward teams whose members move across jobs.

It is important to remember that in the entitlement pay system, employees are assigned to other areas or special projects based upon their past performance. In the entitlement system those who can do are asked to do more. Those who can't or won't are asked to do less. Pay for performance addresses this inequity.

7. Help — Will the organizational structure and resources be in place to enable me to consistently meet the goals?

Employees may feel comfortable in their personal ability to perform. However, they may still be concerned that others in the organization will reduce their opportunity through limiting their ability to perform their job, or through reducing overall organizational profitability. This concern is one of the reasons that only an *organization-wide* system will be perceived as fair and workable by employees.

Cross-functional teams and performance links among dependent departments will also assist in reducing this concern. Ultimately the most convincing demonstration is to implement a no-risk, modest opportunity system that demonstrates that this concern is unfounded or will be overcome.

References

[1] B.F. Skinner. Beyond Freedom and Dignity. New York: Alfred A. Knopf, 1971.

[2] David C. McClelland. *The Achieving Society*. New York: The Free Press, 1961.

"Lease a man a garden
And in time he will leave you
a patch of sand.
Make a man a full owner
Of a patch of sand
and in time he will grow there
A garden on the land."

Index

186

R

S

Smith, 7, 90, 91
social responsibility, 134
span of control, 51
special credit, 178
Sykes, 85
system implementation strategy, 159

T

threshold, 143
time-based pay, 32
time off, 178
Total Performance System, 108, 117
transition strategy, 168
trend analysis, 150
turnaround time, 30
turnover, 156

U

Utilization, 27

V

value-added predictor, 134
variable pay, 95, 101
variance analysis, 151

W

Weber, 10
Weitzman, 17
Whitney, 8
Whyte, 10, 85, 90
working capital efficiency, 132

Z

zero sum game, 48, 53